Silver Charm

Silver Charm

And the Old Friends
Who Save the Thoroughbreds

M.J. Evans

DANCING HORSE PRESS

Copyright © 2025 M.J. Evans

All rights reserved. No part of this publication may be reproduced, distributed or transmitted in any form or by any means, including photocopying, recording, or other electronic or mechanical methods, without the prior written permission of the publisher, except in the case of brief quotations embodied in critical reviews and certain other non-commercial uses permitted by copyright law.

M.J. Evans/Dancing Horse Press
7013 S. Telluride St., Foxfield, CO 80016
www.dancinghorsepress.com

Publishers Cataloging-In-Publication Data
 Name: M.J. Evans, Author Description: Foxfield, Colorado, Dancing Horse Press (2025)/Interest, Age level: 18 and up / Includes bibliographical references. / Summary: Bibliography about the oldest living Kentucky Derby winner, Silver Charm, and the efforts people are making to save the racehorses from slaughter. Subjects: Horses, Horseracing, Horse rescue, Horsemen and Horsewomen, Kentucky Derby, Triple Crown

Ordering information: Special discounts are available on quantity purchases by corporations, associations, and clubs. For details, contact the "Special Sales" department at the address above.

Library of Congress Control Number: 2025909639

 Silver Charm/ M.J. Evans
ISBN: 978-1-7373618-9-3

This book was written by M.J. Evans—not AI

Dedication

Here's to the extraordinary horses—
The ones who are forever woven into our lives,
leaving hoofprints on our hearts.

"I guess I'll always feel something for this horse that I never felt for any other horse I've ridden."
Gary Stevens

Contents

PART 1-CHAMPION
　The Hand of God...9

Marylou Wootton 11
Bob Baffert..14
Bob and Beverly Lewis 18
Gary Stevens 22
Weaving-in Training... 28
The Kentucky Derby 35
The Preakness...47
The Belmont 52
The Eclipse Award 57
Flying in Dubai 60
The Five-Year-Old 67
Sandy Hatfield 71
Living at Three Chimneys.................................77

PART 2-RETIREMENT
　The True Horseman 89

Ferdinand 91
Michael Blowen 96
The Birth of Old Friends Farm 101
Returning home... 108

PART 3-LEGACY
  Saving the Thoroughbreds............................123

John Hettinger 127
Thoroughbred Aftercare Alliance.....................130
California Retirement Management Account . 147
Retired Racehorse Project..............................152

FULL CIRCLE.. 161
In Conclusion: 163
ACKNOWLEDGEMENTS 167
APPENDIX 171
Bibliography 183
  About the Author 189

Part 1
Champion

The Charm

In vibrant hues, our stories weave,
A tapestry that we conceive,
Each thread a laugh, a whispered tear,
A rich design of hope and fear.

With laughter bright and shadows cast,
The colors blend, the die is fast.
In every heart, a pattern grows,
A tapestry where love still flows.

From friendships formed to hearts that break,
We stitch the bonds that time won't shake.
So let us cherish each design,
The woven tales that intertwine.

In quiet corners, threads align,
A tapestry of life's design.
Together woven strong and free,
A work of art—our legacy.

The Hand of God

As I read Bob Baffert's autobiography while doing research for this book, I noticed that he repeatedly referred to fate. He referenced how his life was affected by circumstances that arose despite no specific action of his own. This is what he referred to as "fate."

Some might call these unexpected or unexplained events "coincidences" or "serendipity," while others, including myself, refer to them as "the hand of God." But whatever description you prefer, we all have experienced events that we can't always explain but that change our lives forever.

These experiences are woven like a tapestry to form us into who or what we become. In weaving, the threads stretched vertically over the loom are called warps. They hold the tension while the weaver runs horizontal threads, called weft, across the warp, interlacing the threads to create a beautiful work of art. Some of these threads are dark, bold, maybe even threatening. But they provide the needed contrast to the bright and light threads, adding depth and meaning.

Our lives are like the warp. The people, and even the animals we meet, are the weavers, and their actions are the weft.

The life of the champion Thoroughbred racehorse Silver Charm is one such tapestry, woven by the many people who were placed in his path. As

I write this book, he is living a life of comfort and joy in a large, bluegrass-covered paddock at the Old Friends Farm in Georgetown, Kentucky. He is currently the oldest living Kentucky Derby winner at thirty-one.

This is the story of this remarkable horse's life, and how the people who were instrumental in weaving his life's story brought about his arrival at that lovely green pasture.

CHAPTER 1

Marylou Wootton

In vibrant hues our stories weave

On February 22, 1994, a mare named Bonnie's Poker paced in a large stall, well-padded with a deep layer of straw bedding. She, being a bit ornery, waited for the people to leave. Most mares, ornery or not, prefer to deliver their foals alone. Eighty-six percent of mares, in fact, wait until after the midnight hour to give birth.

Mary Lou Wootton, Bonnie's breeder, split her time between Florida, where her mare was now preparing for delivery at the Ocala-based Dudley Farm, and New York. In New York, she served on the boards of several organizations that helped jockeys and employees in the Thoroughbred racing industry.

Bonnie's Poker had done well in the racing world but was not a standout. To improve the prospect of getting a winning foal, Mrs. Wootton selected a Florida favorite, Silver Buck, when she bred her mare. The stallion was considered the grand patriarch among Florida breeding stallions at the time. Yet, in 1994, this foal, despite being Silver Buck's offspring, would have to make a name for itself on its own, as its pedigree was not considered exceptionally strong.

Mrs. Wootton had hopes for the best.

Bonnie's Poker delivered a dark gray colt with a white blaze down his face and a touch of silver on the tip of his feathery tail. For several months, the colt stayed by his mother's side, Bonnie being a patient mother. The mare allowed her colt to nurse but eventually encouraged him to nibble the grass in the Florida field where they were turned out. By the time the colt turned six months old, he was weaned from his mother and put in a separate paddock.

It was then that humans, and even other horses, began entering Silver Charm's life—the fate that Bob Baffert writes about in his autobiography. The weaving began.

Mrs. Wootton sold her beautiful gray colt as a yearling to a partnership between Randy Hartley and Dean De Renzo for $16,500. The two men were based in Florida and engaged in what is called "pinhooking." That means they specialized in buying young horses, then selling them a short time later, usually privately, for a profit.

Such was the case for this young colt when he was sold right away to a Canadian jockey named Tim Gardiner. Gardiner worked the colt a few times and really liked the way he moved, so he recommended that one of his clients, a man named C.J. Gray, buy him privately before the annual Ocala sale.

Mr. Gray did just that, paying $30,000 for the Charm, and in another "pin-hook," put him up for sale at the Ocala Sale in Ocala, Florida. This sleight-of-hand took place over the course of a year. By this time, Silver Charm was a beautifully developing two-year-old.

But fate, coincidence, or the hand of God was with Silver Charm. As it turned out, Tim Gardiner broke horses for a man named J.B. McKathan, who worked for a young California trainer named Bob Baffert. Baffert just happened to be in a position where he was looking for a good prospect for a client. With the expectation that he would be able to turn around and sell the Charm to one of his clients, Baffert and McKathan went together to buy the colt from C.J. Gray.

Mary Lou Wootton, the woman who started the tapestry of Silver Charm's life, passed away on February 3, 2003, at her home in Long Island, New York. Happily, she lived long enough to see him accomplish great things.

CHAPTER 2

Bob Baffert

A tapestry that we conceive...

If in October 2024 you had looked up "Famous People Born in Nogales, Arizona," you would have found two young TikTok stars that I've never heard of, two old movie stars that I've also never heard of, a musician, and an equestrian. That equestrian I had heard of, and he is indeed famous. His name is Bob Baffert.

Baffert was born in this high desert town of 6,000 near the Mexico border on January 13, 1953. He grew up on a ranch where his father raised cattle and a few horses. Fairly isolated from the rest of civilization, the close-knit family of seven children had only one another to depend upon for entertainment.

Chapter 2 - Bob Baffert

Bob Baffert's love of horses began at a young age, around five or six. He was the only one of his siblings who was drawn to the horses. Eager to get home from school each day, he would run back outside and saddle up.

When Baffert was ten, his father got interested in racing Quarter Horses, a very popular pastime in Arizona to this day. Taking advantage of the mild winters, the Arizona Quarter Horse Association runs its races from the beginning of November all the way to the beginning of May, quitting before the intense heat of summer sets in.

Baffert's father and uncle started buying and breeding Quarter Horses in the early 1960s. The first one put in training was a horse named Baffert's Heller. While Baffert's Heller didn't prove to be a great racehorse, Bob Baffert thought he was the most beautiful horse he had ever seen. When his father pulled Baffert's Heller off the track, he hired a new trainer to prepare him to be a riding horse. I use the term "trainer" very loosely, for once Baffert's Heller was returned to the ranch and Bob started riding him, it took the boy a year to get Baffert's Heller to stop bucking every time he tried to ride him.

As a young equestrian on the ranch, the idea of becoming a jockey had not yet begun sprouting in Baffert's mind. But fertilization of the seed was provided with his father's new involvement in horse racing and the time the young boy spent at the track helping to care for his father's horses. Baffert started riding competitively at the age of eleven, even though his mother strongly opposed it. With his father's support and encouragement, he lived a secret life as a very young jockey. He described this in his autobiography: "We had a deal. I'd never say anything about him drinking beer, and he'd never say anything about me being a jockey."

While in high school, (the time his hair started to prematurely turn its trademark white!) Baffert had his first experience riding Thoroughbreds. Eventually, he realized Thoroughbreds were his future and California was the place he needed to be. Over the next few years of bouncing around, and after finally getting his college degree from the University of Arizona, he chose to put the Quarter Horses aside and focus just on Thoroughbreds—but not as a jockey. He would concentrate on becoming a trainer. (Realize that there is no university you can attend that will teach you how to become a trainer of racehorses. Baffert, like all other trainers, had to come to the racetrack and learn by doing.)

Switching to Thoroughbred racing was a hard decision to make, for Baffert had been remarkably successful in the Quarter Horse racing world as a trainer. His Quarter Horse racing career, during which he trained horses owned by other people, spanned from 1975 to 1991. During that time, his horses earned more than seven million dollars.

By the time Silver Charm came into his life, Bob Baffert was already making a name for himself in the Thoroughbred racing world. The white-haired guy from California was bringing horses to the big races and people were starting to take notice.

Baffert was incredibly newsworthy and was a favorite with sports writers for his outgoing personality. He was willing to talk to reporters and even tell a joke or two. His successes, and even failures, got him the attention he relished.

Then the day came when he received a call from J.B. McKathan.

CHAPTER 3

Bob and Beverly Lewis

Each thread a laugh, a whispered tear...

Bob Baffert had already come to trust J.B. McKathan's ability to scout out four-legged talent, so when his friend called to tell him about the gray colt he'd found, Baffert listened. Not being available to go to Florida himself for the sale, Baffert relied on a tape that McKathan sent him. It was love at first sight. Baffert seemed to have a sixth sense when it came to picking horses. A gift, so to speak. And that sense began to tingle. Just by watching the tape, he knew this horse had what it takes. And he knew he had to have this horse.

By the time Baffert got a hold of McKathan, Silver Charm had already been sold for $100,000. But fate, coincidence, or the hand of God

Chapter 3 - Bob and Beverly Lewis

intervened. The original sale fell through. So, for $80,000 for the horse, and an extra $5,000 for McKathan's finder's fee, the two men became joint owners of Silver Charm.

Now Baffert just needed to find a client to sell him to. As much as he would have loved to keep him for himself, that's a lot of money for a young horse trainer! Baffert's intention was to sell the horse to one of his clients so he could remain the trainer.

As it is often said, "The third time's the charm." Or in this case, "The third time's the Silver Charm." It was the third owner that Baffert approached who agreed to buy him. And with that, Bob and Beverly Lewis became weavers, adding wefts in Silver Charm's tapestry.

With a quick phone call to the Lewises, who were already among his clients, Baffert sold Silver Charm for $85,000. The colt was immediately shipped to Baffert's barn at Santa Anita Park in California. If one could have gotten into Silver Charm's head at that time, it likely would have shown the horse wondering what was to become of him after being shuffled around so much. The Charm was soon to learn that Bob Baffert had a plan for his life, and it involved running—running very fast! And with Bob and Beverly Lewis as the owners, that plan was going to come to fruition.

Bob Lewis got a taste of horse racing in 1946, but it wasn't as an owner. He was a young Californian then, just released from the Army after World War II ended. With $300 in his pocket from the army, he and a friend enjoyed the California sun at the Hollywood Park Racetrack but squandered the money. Once it was gone, Lewis realized it was time to get serious about his future. So, he packed his car and drove up to Eugene, Oregon to attend the University of Oregon.

It was at a local hangout for college students called "College Side Inn" that he first laid eyes on a cute nineteen-year-old coed named Beverly. From the first date, they were committed to one another.

Beverly often snuck out of her sorority house through a window to accompany Lewis on dates to Portland Meadows Racetrack which had opened the year they met. It was a two-hour drive north from the U of O campus.

Perhaps he was able to woo her by his uncanny ability to pick winners. Whatever the reason, the two were married on August 2, 1947.

It seems Beverly was also good at picking a winner. Lewis moved from driving a beer truck in southern California, to becoming the sales manager, to eventually owning the Foothill Beverage Company in Pomona, east of Los Angeles, and later adding the Antelope Valley Distributing Company in Lancaster, CA. Selling beer brewed by Anheuser-Busch, and having an innate business acumen, made him a millionaire.

While work and their three children consumed most of their life together, going to the racetrack remained a favorite pastime for Bob and Beverly Lewis. In 1986, their hobby expanded. Their first dalliance with owning racehorses involved a pacer named Poppa Luigi. Pacers and trotters compete in harness racing and must never break out of a trot.

Chapter 3 - Bob and Beverly Lewis

Getting involved in this type of horse racing simply fueled the passion both were feeling. Three years later, the Lewises invested in their first Thoroughbred racehorse. This modest beginning eventually resulted in owning seventy-two racehorses. Silver Charm was one of several that became champions over the years. The team of Bob and Beverly Lewis was smart enough to hire two of the very best trainers to work for them: first, D. Wayne Lukas, and soon after, Bob Baffert.

Over the many years of their involvement in the world of Thoroughbred racing, the Lewises earned a reputation as good guys. In a business often criticized as populated with crooks and shysters, Bob and Beverly Lewis maintained their values of kindness, respect, and honesty.

When Silver Charm won the Kentucky Derby in 1997, Bob Lewis was quoted as saying: "I've asked Beverly, when she plants me six feet under, to put on that tombstone 'Loving husband, adoring father, and winning owner of the 123rd Kentucky Derby."

And he promised to come back to make sure she did.

CHAPTER 4

Gary Stevens

A rich design of hope and fear...

Bob and Beverly Lewis chose yellow and green silks for their stable in honor of their alma mater. Gary Stevens traveled a long road before donning them aboard Silver Charm at Churchill Downs.

Born in Boise, Idaho, he was the third of three sons, behind brothers Craig and Scott. The latter of those two became an accomplished jockey himself, and later, Gary's coach.

Gary's ideal childhood was marred when, at the age of six, he was diagnosed with Legg-Calve-Perthes disease. This is a rare condition found in children in which the blood vessels do not supply blood to the bones in the hip, and the bone starts to degenerate. Children who are small for their age

Chapter 4 - Gary Stevens

and very active are the most susceptible. So, for a year and a half, Gary had to wear a full leg brace and a built-up shoe to allow the hip bone to regenerate.

Stevens considers it one of several miracles in his life that he was out of the brace in just eighteen months. And he claims the teasing he endured from other kids taught him how to become a fighter. This is a trait he later took into the jockey room on occasion. As a group, jockeys are, pound for pound, some of the toughest customers around! Fight is also a trait that saw Gary Stevens through to the finish line in not only the Run for the Roses but in hundreds of other races as well.

Horses were a big part of the Stevens family. His mother grew up with horses and pulled his father into the equestrian world, first with pleasure horses, then Appaloosa racehorses which led to Quarter Horses, then Thoroughbreds.

The training techniques are dissimilar for each breed because the distances the horses run are different. Quarter Horses are known for being the fastest at a distance of 440 yards, or a quarter of a mile. Appaloosas run that distance and longer because they have more stamina. They can run in races from a quarter mile up to three-quarters of a mile. The latter is the starting length for Thoroughbreds who run that length and longer, up to two miles. The most common race distances in Thoroughbred racing are six furlongs (0.75 miles), 1 mile, and 1 1/8 miles. The Kentucky Derby is a mile and a quarter.

Gary's father eventually maintained a forty-horse stable at Les Bois Park, the Boise racetrack. Ultimately, both Scott and Gary became involved in their father's racing business, taking care of the horses before and after school. Their father continued working at his "real" job—as a manager at Associated Foods. He eventually quit to go into training and racing Quarter Horses full-time.

Gary began riding as a three-year-old on their little acreage in Boise. His first mount was a Shetland pony named Popcorn. (Anyone who knows horses will agree that a Shetland pony will toughen up any child in a hurry!) At six and seven, he did very little with horses due to his brace, but he did learn how to ride a bike using one leg.

Caring for his father's racehorses taught Gary a lot, but it wasn't until he was twelve years old, when a Thoroughbred named Golden Ribbon entered his life, that his outlook changed. Before that time, he hadn't even considered becoming a jockey. Feeling the power of the horse beneath him and through the reins as he exercised Golden Ribbon gave Gary a thrill he had never experienced before. He wrote of the experience in his autobiography: "My first mile and a half gallop on Golden Ribbon, though an isolated event, was decisive. I climbed on that horse because I wanted to do what my brother was doing. I was hooked immediately, and my fear was gone." He discovered his gift for riding horses, and a passion for thrill-seeking.

His brother Scott became his coach, with tips he continued to offer throughout Gary's racing career. For example, from his book: "Keep your heels down." "Keep your weight in your toes." "What helps you maintain your balance is the horse pulling on the bridle and you sitting against the reins." "Keep your left foot slightly in front and your

Chapter 4 - Gary Stevens 25

right foot slightly behind." "Stay relaxed and loose."

While doing my research, I couldn't help but notice the similarity between the childhoods of Bob Baffert and Gary Stevens when it came to an early exposure to horses and horse racing. Similar backgrounds could very well have been a connection that would later bond jockey and trainer. Stevens described the relationship between him and Baffert as being more like brothers.

As a junior in high school, Stevens decided to drop out and work toward becoming a licensed jockey. He was seventeen years old.

But the road to the Derby was not all easy and filled with glory. He suffered some serious injuries that would cause him pain for the rest of his life. One particularly horrendous accident happened when he was training a young filly named Irish Kristen. Starting from the gate, the filly burst out, but other horses being schooled on the track were coming toward her. Seeing the oncoming horses, Irish Kristen tried to take a sharp left-hand turn to change direction. Stevens' saddle slipped right, and he found himself stuck in the stirrups. He never liked getting off a horse going forty miles an hour, but in this case, he couldn't get off even if he had wanted to. The filly hit the rail at chest height, and Stevens went flying over the filly's head and into the infield. Unconscious for thirteen hours, he woke up in the intensive care unit of the hospital. The seriousness of his injuries resulted in several surgeries, weeks in the hospital, and months of physical therapy. (Horse-lovers will be relieved to know that the horse was alright.)

26 *Silver Charm*

No jockey manages a career on the back of a half-ton, living, breathing, volatile animal without suffering numerous injuries. The lucky ones live through them. Not everyone does. Several jockeys have been known to be riding a horse at nearly forty miles per hour when their mount is tripped from behind by an oncoming horse and goes down. The jockey ended up either underneath his own mount, or out on the track in front of a pack of horses bearing down on him. Horse racing is a dangerous sport. *PBS News* reported that the yearly average is two deaths per year and sixty riders beyond that left paralyzed.

Despite the severe injuries Stevens had to overcome, his love of horses and the sport of racing kept him going. Many people doubted that he would ever ride again. But Stevens refused to let go of his goals and ambitions, so ingrained were they. The thrill of riding an eleven- or twelve-hundred-pound Thoroughbred at forty miles an hour was intoxicating.

Four months and a week later, he was back in the saddle, back on the horses, feeling their power as their front legs reached forward to grab the earth. Hearing their breaths come in rhythm with the pounding of their hooves and the beating of their hearts kept him alive.

Even though he was riding again, he found he was struggling to get his confidence back. The encouragement from the older, and renowned, jockey, Bill Shoemaker helped push him forward. Stevens records in *The Perfect Ride* that Shoemaker told him, "Don't worry. You're gonna be all right. In two months, you're gonna be back where you were."

In two months' time, he indeed was near the top again and never looked back.

Before the memorable day when Bob Baffert called and asked him to ride Silver Charm in the races preceding the 1997 Kentucky Derby, Stevens had already won several major races. While still a long way from the more than 5,000 career wins he would eventually amass, he nonetheless was already quite accomplished. He had won the 1988 Kentucky Derby on another gray, that time a filly named Winning Colors—only the third filly to ever win the Kentucky Derby. And he'd won the Kentucky Derby again in 1995, as well as the '95 Belmont, on a big stallion named Thunder Gulch, whom Gary described in his autobiography as a "big playboy."

With Bob Baffert, Bob and Beverly Lewis, and Gary Stevens now weaving together, Silver Charm's life tapestry began to emerge.

CHAPTER 5

Weaving-in Training

With laughter bright and shadows cast...

Once Silver Charm arrived at Bob Baffert's barn at Santa Anita, training began. Baffert created a training chart for Silver Charm that included exactly what was to be done each day. Silver Charm needed to be schooled in several of the racetrack intricacies, from learning how to switch leads at the gallop to how to load into the starting gate.

I learned about the lead changes when I went on a tour of Keeneland Racecourse in Lexington, Kentucky. While watching the early-morning workouts from the rail, I noticed the horses were all on the right lead (leading with the right leg in the canter or gallop) while galloping past those of us standing at the finish line in the middle of the

Chapter 5 - Weaving-in Training 29

straightaway. Yet, the track is built in a large oval, and in America, the horses run in a counterclockwise direction, so the race is run in a left-hand circle.

Silver Charm during a workout on the right lead.
– From Keenland Library Barrett Collection

Curious about this, I asked our tour guide why they were running on the right lead. He didn't know. Actually, he didn't know what I meant when I talked about leads. So, I walked to the end of the track to watch the horses take the turn. Sure enough, one by one the horses switched to the left lead when they entered the turn. Had they not done this "flying change," they would have had to "counter-canter" on the curve, which is much harder for a horse to do. I also learned that if a horse stays on the same lead for the full race, he will become fatigued more quickly.

It is also important to realize that horses don't naturally know how to go into the starting gate and come out of it in a full gallop. While a Tesla electric automobile can go from zero to sixty mph in less than two seconds, don't expect that from a horse. However, getting to their top speed as quickly as possible can make all the difference in the world. Thus, a racehorse needs to be trained to literally burst out of the gate. But before they can be taught that, they must be taught to go into the gate, stand for an indeterminate amount of time, then learn what the bell means when it rings.

I know a little about this from teaching my horses to load into a trailer. If my 1,200-pound horse was too afraid to go in the trailer, I'd never be able to win the argument; I'd never make it to the show or trail.

This is the same for the Thoroughbreds and the starting gates. Try to imagine what the gate would look like to a horse, many of whom are claustrophobic to begin with. So, gate training needs to be done in a slow, step-by-step manner. It begins with simply leading the horse past the gates in both directions. Horses have this unusual brain pattern that causes them to think an object seen from one side of their head is completely unfamiliar when seen from the other side.

Chapter 5 - Weaving-in Training

These are the starting gates that were used when Silver Charm ran in the Kentucky Derby (Photo by the author.)

Once the horse is comfortable walking past the gates from both directions, both the front and the back gates are opened. The horse is led through at a walk repeatedly. It can help to have a young horse follow an experienced horse.

The next step is to close the front gate and lead

the horse in and just let him stand. When he is comfortable standing, the back gate can be closed and the front gate opened. The horse is led out at a walk.

With a rider on his back, the horse can be taught first to walk out of the gate, then trot out, then canter, then burst out into a full gallop. This takes several weeks to accomplish. Most trainers don't take the horse to the starting gate every day as horses can get bored as easily as people. So, they vary their training from day to day.

While talking with Gary Stevens, he made the comment that Silver Charm was always easy about going into the gate without argument. I'm sure this was the result of many weeks of patient training.

Bob Baffert was also a believer in using a soft roll over the noseband of the bridle to keep the horse from shying at the shadows in front of him. The Charm is seen in his races wearing Baffert's traditional blue roll over his nose.

In Baffert's autobiography *Dirt Road to the Derby*, he describes an intriguing small part of Silver Charm's tapestry, the beginning of this incredible horse's life journey. On one occasion, Baffert wrote that he took Silver Charm to Del Mar, the racetrack near San Diego, to work him from the gate. The trainer was thrilled at the elapsed time the Charm brought in at six furlongs. Visions of the Kentucky Derby started dancing in Baffert's head. So, he decided it was time to unleash this as-yet-unraced two-year-old to the real world. He entered him in a six-furlong race on Pacific Classic Day, certain the Charm would win his maiden race. But the Charm was left behind in the mud, and Baffert

Chapter 5 - Weaving-in Training

began thinking, *"Man, was I wrong about him?"*

Baffert called the vet to the barn and had the Charm scoped. He discovered that the horse was a bleeder.

A bleeder is a horse that bleeds from the lungs as a result of strenuous exercise. It is common worldwide in performance horses who compete in events such as racing, eventing, barrel racing, cutting, reining, and roping events. It has even been observed in camel racing and greyhound racing!

Bleeding is defined as the presence of blood in the tracheobronchial tree, which is the system of tubes in the lungs, after strenuous exercise. In other words, blood is leaking into the lungs. During strenuous exercise, the heart rate increases to circulate more oxygenated blood, which raises blood pressure in the capillaries. This can cause microscopic tears in the pulmonary capillaries. With the use of an endoscopic examination of the airways, as many as seventy-five percent of racehorses have been found to be bleeders, but less than five percent bleed from the nose. Thus, it is hard to determine without a vet exam.

At the time, Lasix was the preferred treatment. Subsequently, other treatments gained favor as some races prohibited the use of Lasix. It was found that, because Lasix dehydrates the horse for a short period of time, the horse is at an increased risk of suffering a stroke.

With careful treatment using Lasix, Silver Charm began running the way he was meant to run, and Baffert's visions of the Derby returned.

Not long after Silver Charm started winning some races, Baffert related in his book, that an offer of $1.7 million dollars came in to purchase the Charm. Baffert was heartbroken. While he understood that the Lewises had a hard time turning down so much money, he secretly hoped the sale wouldn't go through.

The day the buyer's agents came to see Silver Charm, Baffert wrote, he told his exercise rider: "Larry, I want you to make him look real shitty today. Don't even carry your stick. I don't want to sell this horse, but I want them to be the ones to back out. When he comes back, I'm going to ask you how he went, and I want you to say he felt okay, but not like he did at Del Mar. Maybe it's the track here. Say it usually takes him about a mile to warm out of it. Just don't go overboard. I don't want it to sound too obvious that we're trying to talk them out of it."

Much to Baffert's relief, a couple of days later, the buyers backed out of the deal.

CHAPTER 6

The Kentucky Derby

The colors blend, the die is fast...

Churchill Downs, Louisville, Kentucky.

Bob Baffert called Gary Stevens in late 1996 when Silver Charm was still a two-year-old and asked him to give the young colt a test ride. Gary, still recovering from shoulder surgery, jumped at the chance. Stevens had ridden against the Charm in the Del Mar Futurity in August of that year. Stevens was riding the $725,000 Gold Tribute, while David Flores was riding the $85,000 Silver Charm, both owned by the Lewises. The Charm won!

Stevens worked Silver Charm one lovely, sunny morning on the track at Santa Anita. Gary jumped off after the workout, and Baffert asked him what he thought of the colt.

"He's a freak," Gary said.

Taken aback, Baffert asked him what he meant.

Gary explained his response in his autobiography, *The Perfect Ride*. "What it meant, I guess, was that Silver Charm impressed me with his energy and alertness, and as I worked him, it became clear that he could do things no other two-year-old could do at that stage. The colt had speed, but when I asked him, he would show even more speed—not all of his speed, maybe just half. I sensed that much more was there."

After that fateful call from Baffert, offering him the chance to ride the Charm, Stevens stepped in and took the reins, literally. The jockey started following Baffert's instructions about how hard and how long to work him.

Over the next few months, Gary Stevens and Bob Baffert learned that Silver Charm was basically lazy. He would work only as hard as he needed to, and no more.

The other issue was his bleeding. He came in from a race breathing very hard. X-rays showed he had some scar tissue in one lung. Baffert hypothesized that he must have had pneumonia when he was young. "Either that or he once spent a summer in a Kentucky coal mine," Baffert wrote as a joke in *The Dirt Road to the Derby*. But the blowing was so pronounced, it scared away his previous jockey.

Chapter 6 - The Kentucky Derby 37

*(Gary Stevens on Silver Charm -
Keeneland Library Barrett Collection)*

In 1997, it was much easier to qualify for a spot in the Kentucky Derby field than it is today. Winnings for races a horse ran, even as a two-year-old, counted toward the horse's total. And races of all grades, whether a Grade 1, Grade 2, or Grade 3 race, could be counted. This old system meant that Churchill Downs had no say as to which horses could qualify for the race. A horse could earn enough money on shorter races or even races on turf and show up for the Derby wholly unqualified to run. This tended to undermine the performance of the horses that were truly prepared and deserving to be there.

This all changed way after Silver Charm's time. Beginning in 2013, the field for the Derby is determined by the 20 horses (plus two on a waiting list in case of a scratch) that earned the most points at predetermined races. Races outside the United States are even counted now.

In an interview for the *Paulick Report* in 2017, Gary Stevens lamented the fact that the field is now so large. He believes that it is too dangerous to run twenty horses and believes that the field size should be reduced to fourteen as it is in the Preakness. At this writing, the field is still twenty.

Back in the spring of 1997, Silver Charm was finally prepared for the Santa Anita Derby, one of the races that now qualifies a horse for the Kentucky Derby but at that time simply offered a large enough purse to help a horse get there. Losing by a head to Free House didn't dampen Baffert's or Stevens' spirits one bit, as a second-place finish still brought in a lot of money.

But, perhaps more importantly, the race showed Stevens just how talented Silver Charm was. The times for each quarter of the mile-and-one-eighth race were much faster than he expected. It didn't feel to Stevens like the Charm was straining at all. He knew he had a real athlete under him; the jockey relished the feeling of nearly effortless power Silver Charm displayed.

"I learned something important from Silver Charm that day—that he could be a very versatile horse. I didn't need to rush him; he didn't have to run near the lead. I could use his speed tactically to put him into a race but save his best for the final quarter of a mile . . . my colt put enormous pressure

Chapter 6 - The Kentucky Derby

on Sharp Cat and still had enough left to put in a grueling last two furlongs," he wrote in *The Perfect Ride*. He told me during our interview that he knew they may have lost the battle, but they would win the war.

The Twin Spires were now in sight. Feeling confident, they put Silver Charm on a plane and flew off to Louisville.

It has been said that the thrill of victory is not as powerful as the disappointment of defeat. Bob Baffert had watched his horse, Cavonnier, lose the 1996 Kentucky Derby to Grindstone in a photo finish. It still stung at the very thought. Now, after such a painful disappointment the year before, Baffert was back in Louisville. In *Dirt Road to the Derby* he wrote that, as he walked the grounds, he said to himself, "I've got to win this race. If it takes me the rest of my life, I've got to win this race."

Silver Charm and his team arrived ten days before the Derby. The Charm was housed with the other Derby contenders in Barn 42, the shedrow at the back of the grounds. This barn had the distinction of being called "The Derby Barn." In 1973, the famous Secretariat was housed in one of these stalls. A wall separated the row of stalls from the busy streets and tiny, rundown homes of the section of Louisville that bordered the grounds of Churchill Downs.

Silver Charm watched the goings-on from over his stall door, his ears twitching as he took in both the familiar and the unfamiliar sounds: horses nickering and stomping in their stalls, birds chirping in the overhanging branches of the trees, grooms and jockeys comparing their mounts . . .

and over the walls, the sounds of dogs barking, children playing, and traffic in the street.

The shedrows at any racetrack are a world of their own. The smell of hay and manure fills the air as the people who live and work on the backside—the ones who really know the horses best—go about their daily chores of feeding, watering, grooming, bathing, shoeing, and exercising their charges. And doing it all again the next day and the next, and the ones after that.

Early morning workouts commenced for Silver Charm. But the bleeding continued, even with the Lasix treatments. The vet gave Silver Charm one day's worth of antibiotics to forestall any infection, but Baffert was nervous. He was afraid Silver Charm would get sick right before the Derby. Living in fear those last few days, Baffert had Silver Charm's temperature taken every few minutes to make sure he wasn't getting sick.

Derby Day, always the first Saturday in May, dawned cold and miserable in 1997. But while the weather looked foreboding, Silver Charm looked confident. Nothing was bothering him; nothing was causing him to become nervous or excited. In *Dirt Road to the Derby,* Baffert described him this way: "One thing about this horse, he is so cool. He's got ice water in his veins." In fact, the horse was so relaxed, Baffert feared that the Charm might be getting sick. The vet administered a dose of Lasix to prevent the bleeding.

Silver Charm's groom prepared him for the race by carefully currying and brushing his coat and braiding his forelock and top part of his mane. Then Baffert, preferring to saddle his horses himself,

Chapter 6 - The Kentucky Derby 41

took the line and led Silver Charm away from the barn. The most exciting two minutes in sports was about to begin!

The Run for the Roses, as the Kentucky Derby is known because the winning horse is draped in a blanket of red roses in the Winner's circle, is the biggest event of the year in Louisville. A few years later, attendees would enter the grounds by passing a historical marker that reads:

CHURCHILL DOWNS

Home of the Kentucky Derby, the oldest continuously held sporting event in America, for 3-year-old thoroughbreds. Aristides, owned by H.P. McGrath & ridden by black jockey Oliver Lewis, won the 1st Derby in 1875. Meriwether Lewis Clark Jr., grandson of explorer Wm. Clark, named and modeled the KY. Derby after English Epson Derby.
Presented by the Kentucky Derby Museum.

42 *Silver Charm*

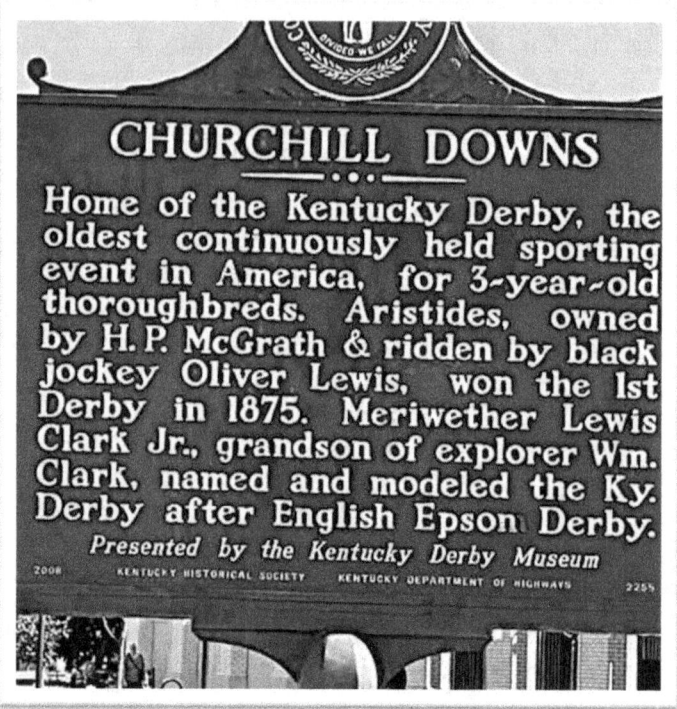

(Photo by the author)

Even with the less-than-desirable weather, the stands and the infield were filled with racegoers—141,981 in all. Rich, poor, black, white, old, young—they all blended together to enjoy the event. Ladies, in their colorful hats, sipped mint juleps while their husbands argued over which horse to bet on. Captain Bodgit was the odds-on favorite, but Silver Charm was getting his share of attention.

The horses are taken to the paddock in the order of their position in the starting gate. Passing through the tunnel to the paddock, Baffert felt Silver Charm get focused. The horse seemed to puff

Chapter 6 - The Kentucky Derby

up his chest to let the world know he was there. The Charm knew just what he needed to do. Sensing the change in Silver Charm, the trainer felt his confidence return. His horse was ready to run the mile-and-a-quarter race. Baffert led his horse to his saddling stall to tack him up.

In *Dirt Road to the Derby*, Baffert described what followed. Bob saddled him up and turned to Gary. "Just make that move and get us to the front at the eighth pole." Lifting the jockey into the saddle, he added, "Just go out there and do what you got to do. And if we don't make it, we'll just bring another one next year." His last comment belied the pressure he felt to win.

Both jockey and trainer knew the importance of meticulous planning but there was no getting away from the importance of spontaneity. The events in any given race were difficult to predict ahead of time.

One by one, the horses left the paddock. As the first horse stepped onto the track, a bugler, dressed in a red coat and black hat, played the familiar notes of "Called to the Post." As the parade of contenders began, the crowd sang the traditional song, "My Old Kentucky Home."

Thirteen horses were paraded past the grandstands, their jockeys' colorful silks standing out like jewels against the gray sky, sparkling clean now but soon to be soiled by the wet earth. The people in the infield jostled one another for the best vantage point. The rain had eased to a mist that fell softly on all who watched the historic events unfolding before them. With Baffert riding his favored palomino, he ponied Silver Charm and

Stevens as close to the starting gate as they were allowed. The thirteen excited contenders got in position, taking turns loading into the gate.

At the sound of the bell, the gates burst open and Silver Charm broke clean, a relief to Baffert and Bob and Beverly Lewis, who were watching from the stands, surrounded by screaming onlookers. Running from the sixth gate (the first gate was empty) meant Stevens had to take Silver Charm behind the front runners to get closer to the rail. As on most races where the track is muddy, Stevens started the race with several sets of goggles over his eyes. It wasn't long before the top set was splattered with mud from the sloppy track. He had to reach up and pull the first set below his chin, giving him a clear view of the horses ahead. After some such races, the horse's chest would be so covered in mud, the grooms would have to peel the mud off like a second skin.

The crowd in the grandstand cheered as the horses, with tails flying, raced past the iconic Twin Spires for the first of two passes. Silver Charm quickly reached his stride, settling in comfortably, with Stevens perched on the Charm's back, his arms moving forward and back as though a rower on a scull. Temporarily penned between horses and running in fourth place, Silver Charm felt the touch of Stevens' whip as an opening appeared ahead. This is where the skill of a jockey makes such a difference. Stevens had to know if Silver Charm had the ability to get through the opening before it disappeared. With only the slightest encouragement, the determined horse stretched out his forelegs, gripped the muddy track and

Chapter 6 - The Kentucky Derby

pulled himself forward. The world around them became a blur as the Charm rushed through the narrow gap. Bob Baffert jumped to his feet in the stands, yelling "Come on, come on." But his words were drowned out by the cacophony around him.

By the one-mile post, Stevens guided the Charm around the front runners, willing to take a longer route. Silver Charm put on a burst of speed and took the lead. The Charm and Stevens were moving as one, their breathing and heartbeats in sync. Captain Bodgit came up on the outside, but Silver Charm refused to let him get in front.

At this point Stevens felt he was just along for the ride and let himself revel in the feeling of sitting atop the source of such extreme power. With a final surge of strength, Silver Charm pushed forward. The two horses crossed the finish line with the Charm ahead by a neck.

The race announcer shouted into the microphone, "One hundred and twenty-three years and you don't get a better race than this!"

Stevens turned his horse around and cantered past the grandstand, only now cognizant of the cheering crowd. He steered Silver Charm toward the Winner's Circle as photographers snapped their pictures and the spectators roared their approval.

Stevens brought the Charm to a halt in the Winner's Circle and was immediately surrounded by dignitaries and a jubilant Bob Baffert, and Bob and Beverly Lewis. Even though he and the horse were both covered with mud and sweat, Stevens' grin filled his entire face, jubilation falling over his shoulders like a mantle. The garland of roses was placed over Silver Charm's gray neck.

The design of the garland was first introduced in 1932 and remained unchanged through 2025. There are 426 red roses on the actual blanket, each in its own little vial of water. The edge of the blanket is covered in green ferns. The garland of roses is two and a half yards long and fourteen inches wide. The center crown, which rests on the horse's withers, holds the number of long-stemmed red roses representing each horse that ran in that year's race. The garland weighs a whopping forty pounds. Add to that, the jockey is presented with a bouquet of sixty long-stemmed roses wrapped in ten yards of red ribbon. The scent of all those roses would surely remain in Gary Stevens' memory for the rest of his life.

The celebration over Silver Charm winning the Kentucky Derby went on for days, Baffert relates in *Dirt Road to the Derby*. Friends from way back in high school called to congratulate him. One high school friend told him that a girl they both knew from school responded by saying, "Do you believe it? Do you believe Bobby Baffert, that clown we went to school with, just won the Kentucky Derby?"

That night, all Baffert could think was that his life was fulfilled. But there was still more to come for him and Silver Charm. Many people doubted that Silver Charm had the ability to sustain such a performance in the Preakness. But the Charm's weavers were not among them.

CHAPTER 7

The Preakness

In every heart, a pattern grows...

Pimlico Racecourse, Baltimore, Maryland
The trip to Pimlico Racecourse in Baltimore for the Preakness was a different story than how things had been leaving California for Louisville. Baffert felt like the weight of the world had been lifted; he was much more relaxed. Even though Silver Charm's workouts were sluggish, Baffert wasn't worried. There were two weeks between the big races, and Silver Charm seemed healthy. The trainer enjoyed himself while in Baltimore. He even attended an Orioles versus Seattle Mariners baseball game, where he threw out the ceremonial first pitch before a cheering crowd.

The entire team felt confident in Silver Charm's

abilities.

Stevens was being careful about his weight, a constant struggle for him and most jockeys, and he was making daily hot box visits to sweat off the pounds. He weighed himself upwards of forty times a day. His maximum weight was 115 pounds. He was more worried about maintaining his weight than he was about Silver Charm's capability.

On the day of the race, Bob Baffert's white hair made him easy to spot in a crowd. As he led Silver Charm to the paddock, the crowd called out to both Baffert and Silver Charm with cheers and words of encouragement. Many had put their money on the Charm.

Gary Stevens rarely rode Silver Charm during exercise time. So, when he showed up, Silver Charm knew him and knew it was showtime. Wearing the green and yellow striped silks of the Lewises' stable, Stevens mounted Silver Charm in the paddock. Once in the saddle, Gary felt at peace. If you work at something long enough, hard enough, it defines your identity. Gary Stevens was a jockey. This was where he belonged.

Stevens appreciated that Baffert gave him very little instruction before the race and let him run the race as it played out. The trainer's way of dealing with his nervousness before the race was to tell jokes. This was another of the many things Stevens valued about working with Baffert.

The 122nd running of the Preakness Stakes took place on May 17, 1997. As the second jewel of the Triple Crown, the race covered a mile and three-sixteenths. Unlike the rain-soaked Kentucky Derby,

Chapter 7 - The Preakness

race day at Pimlico was bright and sunny, with a dry, fast track. The stands were packed with eager fans, anticipating another thrilling showdown between the two gray California rivals, Silver Charm and Free House.

Silver Charm was in the sixth position, as he had been in the Derby, but this time only ten horses were waiting for the gates to spring open. Cryp Too was being uncooperative about loading into the ninth gate. Stevens slowly breathed in and out, keeping himself and his horse calm. The Charm's skin quivered. Stevens rubbed Silver Charm's neck and waited, concentrating on the gates, his eyes on the wide, empty track ahead.

The moment Cryp Too settled into the gate, the doors burst open with a resounding bang. Silver Charm lunged forward, the vast stretch of dirt track unfolding before him. Meanwhile, Touch Gold stumbled badly, nearly going down. Cryp Too surged ahead, seizing a commanding early lead, but his momentum was short-lived as he quickly faded.

As Cryp Too fell back, Free House took the lead while Silver Charm broke from the pack and came up on the outside. With his nose bobbing up and down he reached Free House's hip, then shoulder, then neck and, finally, Silver Charm came up even with Free House. Stride for stride, the two grays eyed each other, their jaws set with determination. In the stands, the crowd roared its approval.

Stevens, acutely aware of Free House pressing beside him, kept his gaze steady between Silver Charm's ears, focused on the open track ahead. As they edged forward, the tension mounted. Barreling down the homestretch, Captain Bodgit mirrored his late charge from the Kentucky Derby, surging up the outside. But Silver Charm's relentless spirit refused to yield, determined to deny Captain Bodgit the lead.

At the same time, the jockey's role in bringing home a winner cannot be over emphasized. With his weight balancing on two narrow strips of metal called stirrups, Stevens rounded his back and lowered his body over The Charm's withers. His grip on the reins tightened almost imperceptibly. The will to win moved like a wave of electricity down the reins, and Silver Charm stretched forward. More than one hundred thousand people watched as Silver Charm pushed ahead and won the second jewel in the Triple Crown by a nose in a photo finish with Free House and Captain Bodgit.

The race was described by sportswriter Jay Friedman this way: "Those qualities of will and heart carried Silver Charm to the brink of immortality with his heart-stopping, photo-finish wins over Free House and Captain Bodgit in the Kentucky Derby and Preakness. Especially the Preakness, in which he seemed to hurl himself at the wire in one final jump when it looked as if Free House was not going to yield."

Touch Gold made a remarkable comeback after his stumble at the gate, recovering enough ground to finish fourth, showing the talent that would come back to haunt Silver Charm at their next meeting.

But that day, it was Silver Charm that stood in the Winner's Circle with a grinning Stevens on his back. As his trainer and owners crowded around him the eight-foot-long blanket of yellow flowers was placed over the Charm's shoulders. The blanket was made the day before by the florists at The Giant food chain and was made of thousands of bright yellow flowers that look like Black-eyed Susans, Maryland's state flower. However, the florists do not use Black-eyed Susan flowers because those don't start blooming until the end of June. Instead, they use Viking mums, which also have the advantage of being larger.

As soon as Silver Charm was officially declared the winner, a painter ascended a ladder to the top of a replica of the Old Clubhouse cupola, which stands proudly in the Winner's Circle on the infield. The original clubhouse, lost to a fire in 1966, left behind only its iron weathervane, now preserved in the museum. The current weathervane, crafted from aluminum, carries on the legacy. With steady hands, the painter carefully applied green and yellow paint to the jockey and gray to the horse—a vivid tribute to the champion. This iconic tradition, which began in 1909, ensures that each year's Preakness winner is honored in lasting color until the next running of the Preakness adds a new chapter in the history of the race.

CHAPTER 8

The Belmont

A tapestry where love still flows...

Belmont Park, Elmont, New York

Silver Charm was making a believer of those who doubted him. He went to the Belmont Stakes, held at Belmont Park in Elmont, New York, as the favorite. The classic race is run over the distance of a mile and a half. It is interesting to note that each of the races in the Triple Crown are of different lengths, thus requiring different skills of the horse. The Belmont is the longest, and truly a test of endurance for the horses. That is why it is called "The Test of Champions."

Chapter 8 - The Belmont 53

*(Silver Charm dressed for a race.
Keeneland Library Barrett Collection)*

The day before leaving Louisville for New York, Bob Baffert went on a radio show and publicly invited everyone who was listening to watch the Charm's final workout. The next day, there was a traffic jam to get into the parking lot. Thousands of people came to watch their hero. Everyone was rooting for the big gray with the white blaze on his face to become the next Triple Crown winner. There had not been a Triple Crown winner since Affirmed—nineteen years earlier.

Before leaving Churchill Downs, Gary Stevens was more tense than usual. He felt an obligation not only to Bob Baffert, the Lewises and Silver Charm, but also to the whole sport of horse racing. It seemed the entire country was on the edge of its seats, hoping for another Triple Crown winner. He didn't want to let anyone down.

As the horses lined up in the starting gate that June 7th, Bob Baffert was in the stands passing out pins that said, "Bet the farm on the Charm."

In the gate, Stevens threaded his fingers through the reins, peered up between his horse's ears and waited. As the bell rang and the gates sprung open, Silver Charm leaped forward, quickly taking the lead. The dry track made for easy going, and Stevens sat comfortably on top. But the lead position didn't belong to Silver Charm for long. Wild Rush pushed ahead, taking over as the front runner. On the first turn, the Charm swung wide, moving over behind Wild Rush, and leaving an opening for Touch Gold to take the lead on the rail. Silver Charm fell back to a tight third place as Wild Rush followed his stablemate, Touch Gold, and started running in the second position.

On the back stretch, Touch Gold fell back as Wild Rush retook the lead. But Silver Charm, not to be denied, came up on the outside, and for a short time, it seemed like it would be a two-horse race. But Free House, who also loved a good challenge, came charging up on the outside. For several

Chapter 8 - The Belmont

strides, there was a wall of three horses, with Silver Charm in the middle. But a threat was lurking behind them. On the final turn, Touch Gold moved around them on the outside, going wide as they came down the home stretch.

An eighth of a mile from the finish, Silver Charm held a comfortable half-length lead over his nearest challenger, Free House, and jockey Gary Stevens felt victory was all but certain—signed, sealed, and delivered. But as they thundered past the sixteenth pole, a flicker of movement caught Stevens' eye.

Silver Charm, running tight to the rail, remained unaware of the threat looming in the middle of the track. The other striking gray, Free House, unwittingly acted as a shield, blocking Silver Charm's view of the oncoming danger.

And then, in the blink of an eye, it was over.

In a mere three seconds, Touch Gold surged past, his powerful stride carrying him under the wire half a length ahead. The dream of a Triple Crown vanished in an instant. The blanket of white carnations would not rest on Silver Charm's shoulders.

The crowd erupted. Surely, most people felt a touch of disappointment that 1997 would not be a year that held a Triple Crown winner. Only those who had bet on Touch Gold were thrilled.

In the stands, Bob Lewis, the true gentleman that he was, thanked Bob Baffert for getting them this close, shouting over the cacophony that exploded all around them. Baffert had enjoyed every minute of the Triple Crown races and was still glowing from the excitement of it all. But out on the track, bringing his horse down to a slow canter, then a trot, Stevens was crushed. He described it this way in *The Perfect Ride:*

"I went from having the highest high I've ever had to the lowest low, an incredible mood swing. I was in a stupor for days—months even—to have come that close to winning the Triple Crown and not to have had it happen. It was something I don't think I'll ever get over; the memory will never go away. After losing that race, I went into a deep, deep depression."

Stevens was sure that, had the Charm seen Touch Gold, he would not have let him get ahead. Silver Charm didn't like to be bested and had both the heart and the ability to win. Out of twenty-four career starts, Silver Charm's wins were never by a large margin. He preferred to just get his nose ahead—more exciting for the cheering crowds.

CHAPTER 9

The Eclipse Award

From friendships formed to hearts that break…

On April 1, 1764, Western Europe and a part of northern Africa experienced an annular eclipse. That is an eclipse where the moon moves between the sun and the Earth when it is at its farthest point from our home planet. The result is that the moon appears smaller than the sun, with a bright solar ring around it. This day, the eclipse was particularly long, lasting six minutes and twenty seconds.

While people in England were talking about and observing the phenomenon, a chestnut colt with one white stocking and a stripe down his face was born at Keats Gore in Berkshire. The colt was a grandson of the Godolphin Arabian, one of the three foundation studs for the English Thoroughbred (the others being the Byerly Turk and the Darley Arabian). In honor of the momentous event, the colt was named "Eclipse." The colt grew to become one of the greatest racehorses of all time, going undefeated in all of his eighteen races.

He began his racing career at the age of five over courses that were typically four miles long. He ran several heats at that length in a day. No horse could beat him. In fact, none even came close. He left the other horses behind by ten to twenty lengths.

Eclipse by George Stubbs
(Alamy Art Collection used with permission)

Eclipse was so fast that his very existence reshaped the study of equine anatomy. In 1792, Britain's Royal Veterinary College—the first school of veterinary medicine in England—was founded in

Chapter 9 - The Eclipse Award

part to examine his skeleton, searching for the secret behind his extraordinary speed. Despite standing a modest sixteen-and-a-half hands with unremarkably long legs, Eclipse defied expectations, dominating every race he entered. His legacy extends far beyond his victories—today, an astonishing 95% of all Thoroughbreds can trace their lineage back to him.

More than two hundred years later, this famous racehorse added to the tapestry of Silver Charm's life.

The Eclipse Award is named after that very same eighteenth-century English racehorse. The award program is the American Thoroughbred horse racing equivalent of the Hollywood Academy Awards. The Eclipse Awards, in their format at the time of this writing, 2025, were founded in 1971—the winners in each division are decided by three organizations: The National Thoroughbred Racing Association, The Daily Racing Form, and the National Turf Writers Association. At a black-tie affair held in January of the following year, winners in the twenty categories are announced.

In January of 1998, the 1997 Eclipse Award for Champion Three-Year-Old Male went to Silver Charm. His trainer, Bob Baffert, received the 1997 Eclipse Award for Outstanding Trainer.

CHAPTER 10

Flying in Dubai

We stitch the bonds that time won't shake...

On the first Monday in August 1997, at Saratoga Racecourse in Saratoga Springs, New York, Gary Stevens was inducted into the Racing Hall of Fame, Thoroughbred racing's highest honor. At that time, he was thirty-four years old and had been riding professionally since his teens. He had won more than 4,000 races, including three Kentucky Derbys. His winnings totaled more than $160 million, of which 10 percent was his.

But his time with Silver Charm was not over yet. The jockey had more to add to the tapestry of Silver Charm's life.

By the start of the 1998 racing season, Silver Charm, Bob Baffert, and Gary Stevens were the most recognized faces in Thoroughbred racing. As

Chapter 10 - Flying in Dubai

people have a tendency to do, some voiced skepticism that Silver Charm was truly a great horse. But the Thoroughbred proved the naysayers wrong by galloping into his four-year-old races with aplomb. At the beginning of 1998, he won two major stakes races at Santa Anita Racetrack. An abscess in a hoof kept him out of the Santa Anita Handicap, but that gave the Charm a ten-day vacation that might have been just what he needed for his next major race: The Dubai World Cup.

Baffert was concerned about one thing as they prepared to fly to Dubai with the Charm. He had still been getting shots of Lasix to control the bleeding. Lasix was a legal drug in the United States; however, it was not legal in Dubai. Baffert didn't know how the absence of the drug would affect his horse.

Another concern for the entire team was the fact that Silver Charm was to be the first Kentucky Derby winner in a long time to race outside the U.S. He would be an ambassador of sorts, and this put an additional layer of pressure on everyone...except the horse!

Added to these concerns was the uncertainty about how the Charm would handle the thirty-six-hour-long trip to the other side of the world. They planned to fly first to Frankfurt, Germany, and from there to Dubai. The Charm was loaded into a four-sided box, then hoisted up into the belly of the plane. In the planes that are set up to transport horses, there can be sixty to eighty horses in a single plane! Grooms travel in the large compartment in the back of the plane with their horses.

I saw a funny meme on the internet once. It

said: "Dogs have owners, Horses have staff!" The truthfulness of that made me laugh. Consider Silver Charm. He has owners, trainers, exercise riders, jockeys, grooms, farriers, vets, and many more people who hover around him at all times. There isn't much he can do without someone noticing. And many of those people got on the plane to fly with him to Dubai. As my six-year-old granddaughter told me after helping me feed our horses: "Teamwork makes the dreamwork."

Upon landing in Frankfurt, Silver Charm was unloaded, given a chance to stretch his legs, offered water, and then reloaded for the final leg of the journey.

Once in Dubai, Silver Charm was given several liters of electrolytes by intravenous injection. This was intended to stave off the effects of jet lag. However, while interviewing Gary Stevens, I learned that horses are not really as affected by jet lag as their handlers thought they would be. Horses aren't on the same sleeping pattern that humans are. In other words, their bodies don't get into a rhythm of eight or more hours of sleep followed by a long waking period. Horses sleep for short periods all through a twenty-four-hour day. This is called a polyphasic sleep pattern. Horses will sleep for fifteen to thirty minutes several times throughout the day and night. They sleep for a total of just two to five hours a day. This was a survival technique inherited from the time when horses were in the wild.

Add to the short sleep segments the fact that horses can sleep standing up, and you have another survival technique. The knees and hocks on a horse

Chapter 10 - Flying in Dubai

can lock and prevent them from falling over. This is called the "Stay Apparatus." There is a group of tendons and ligaments in the horse's legs that work together so the horse can remain standing with little effort. As a prey animal, horses in the wild need to be able to flee quickly if threatened. Awakening from a standing position certainly helps them to be able to do this.

So, the long flight to Dubai was more an issue for the humans than for Silver Charm.

Bob Baffert was surprised when he got off the plane in Dubai. Everything was much different than he expected. Before oil brought wealth to the region, the Emirates didn't exist. The region was nothing more than a desert occupied by roaming tribes on their beautiful Arabian horses. Baffert related in his autobiography that his first sighting, after stepping off the plane, was of a soldier carrying an Uzi machine gun. "I said to him, 'Hey you must be a bad shot if you got an Uzi.' He didn't think that was very funny." But beyond that, Baffert was very impressed with the beauty and cleanliness of Dubai. The architecturally beautiful skyscrapers, for which the city has become famous, were just being plotted and built. Baffert even noted the luxurious, air-conditioned stall into which Silver Charm was led, comparing it to a horse's version of the Ritz.

The Dubai World Cup was first run in 1996 with the horses competing for the astronomical sum of $4 million. The first Dubai World Cup was won by Cigar, winner of Horse of the Year in America in both 1995 and 1996. Silver Charm was participating in only its third running. The race was started by Sheikh Mohammed bin Rashid Al Maktoum, Vice President and Prime Minister of the UAE and Ruler of Dubai. The Sheikh owns one of the world's leading Thoroughbred breeding and racing operations, named for two of the famous Arabian stallions who form the foundation of today's Thoroughbred horses, the Darley Stables and the Godolphin Stables.

Nad Al Sheba Racecourse was the site of the Dubai World Cup. The racecourse had both a dirt track and a turf track, and both tracks were run in a left-hand pattern. The infield, home to a golf course, was once used for the filming of the movie, *Star Trek and Beyond*. The track on which Silver Charm ran was later replaced by a newer, fancier version that is named the Meydan Racecourse.

After days of celebration with Sheikh Mohammed, race day finally arrived. But as Bob Baffert led Silver Charm to the paddock, his heart sank. The colt's head drooped; his lower lip hung slack. He looked as if he were half-asleep.

Then Gary Stevens swung into the saddle.

In an instant, Silver Charm came to life. As Stevens put it, the colt knew his jockey, and he knew exactly what that meant—showtime.

Stevens rode the Charm into the outside gate while nine horses lined up. His horse was awake and alert, dancing on his toes. The track ahead was dry and fast. As the Charm jostled around in the starting gate, waiting for the gates to slam open, Stevens put aside his concerns about representing the United States racing establishment, and focused on the race ahead.

Chapter 10 - Flying in Dubai

With a clang, the gates snapped open and the Charm, in his outside position on the track, dug in his hooves, lowered his hindquarters, and took off. Stevens certainly didn't have a sleepy horse underneath him anymore.

With nine horses barreling down the track, the Charm stayed on the outside, running near the front in second and third around the backside. With a half mile to go, Silver Charm shifted gears. Down the home stretch, Stevens gave the Charm one tap of his whip and the horse leaped in front. Passed briefly on the inside, Stevens switched his whip to the right hand and, with a rhythmic swing of his arm, pushed his horse even faster.

The jockey stayed up out of the saddle to let the horse stretch out. Retaking the lead, the pair was challenged at the last minute by Swain, the horse owned by the Sheikh. Silver Charm was known for making heart-stopping finishes. The Charm was declared the winner in more photo finishes than he lost. The Dubai World Cup was no exception. Silver Charm stretched his long legs and neck forward and won by a sixteenth of an inch. But a nose is all it takes to be the champion!

Stevens said in his autobiography, *The Perfect Ride*, "It was one of the bravest performances made by any horse I have ever ridden."

It was Silver Charm who came home with the $4 million dollar prize. Needless to say, the flight home was one long party for the humans and several long naps for Silver Charm.

Silver Charm won six of his nine starts as a four-year-old, giving him the top spot for earnings at $4,696,508. This helped bump Baffert to the top spot of earnings for trainers, and Gary Stevens to the top spot of earnings for jockeys. His team had millions of reasons to love Silver Charm!

CHAPTER 11

The Five-Year-Old

Together woven strong and free...

After arriving back home in Santa Anita, Silver Charm was given a nice long rest. He took advantage of the time off to get pleasantly fat, a condition he enjoyed. Then Baffert took him to Kentucky to show him off, treating him like the oversized pet that he was.

As a special surprise for the Lewises, Bob Baffert arranged for a professional photographer to capture a one-of-a-kind portrait—but this was no ordinary Thoroughbred headshot.

Draped in the Arabian garb gifted to him in Dubai, Baffert sat astride Silver Charm, wearing a flowing white dishdashi and a red-checked keffiyeh. Vibrant tassels adorned the colt's gray sides and bridle, while an embroidered saddle pad and blanket added to the striking ensemble.

Positioned perfectly on the Churchill Downs track, with the iconic Twin Spires towering in the background, the photographer captured a breathtaking image—one that blended the legacy of a champion with the spirit of the desert.

According to Baffert, Silver Charm was not particularly pleased with the whole situation. Having seen the picture, I can tell just by looking at it that the Charm was not thrilled. Rather than standing and posing, head up, ears alert, he had his head down, his feet dancing with impatience.

When in racing form, Silver Charm was all horse without an ounce of surplus. But after his well-earned vacation, he had become a bit soft. Some horses lose their drive and never get back the competitive heart that will push them to win. Such was not the case with Silver Charm. He came back from his vacation to win two major stakes races. But then he was beaten in the Breeders' Cup Classic by Awesome Again. Stevens describes the loss this way: "He ran a gallant race but lost by less than a length, which was a switch. Usually, he found a way to have his nose in the front at the finish line." Stevens recognized the horse's innate power and willingness. The Charm wanted to win. Often, all Stevens had to do was let him.

In January of 1999, the National Thoroughbred Racing Association (NTRA) was teaming up with the FOX television network to produce the first "Champions on Fox" series for heavyweights. That was the previous term for older horses. The Lewises, knowing what a celebrity Silver Charm was, wanted to support the effort by

Chapter 11 - The Five-Year-Old

having Silver Charm in the race. So, they convinced Bob Baffert to fly the Charm back to his birth-state for the race set in south Florida.

Silver Charm became the big draw for the race. The stallion was given a police escort as he was trailered from the airport to the track. The NTRA set up a tent with Silver Charm memorabilia and keepsakes. All the promotions featured the gray stallion.

But the Donn, the name given to the first in a sequence of 11 races billed by the National Thoroughbred Racing Association as its championship series for senior stars, was not a happy experience for Team Silver Charm. Baffert was upset at the 126 pounds assigned to Silver Charm—6 to 16 pounds more than any of the other competitors. Gary Stevens was upset about the post position they drew three days before the race. They had the outside gate of the twelve horses in the race. So, Silver Charm would have to run a longer distance while carrying more weight. All of these factors worked together to result in a third-place finish for the Charm.

A few months later, Silver Charm was taken back to Dubai for the 1999 Dubai World Cup. The five-year-old was the favorite. But the bleeding problem had become worse.

Lined up in the third gate, Silver Charm and seven other horses waited for the gates to spring open for the world's richest race—a prize of $5 million. The Charm burst from the gate and joined the other horses as they dug in their hooves and sprinted onto the track. He moved to the rail and remained there for most of the race. Coming down the home stretch, Stevens guided him to the middle of the track, but the familiar shift of gears just wasn't there. Silver Charm came in a disappointing sixth.

Silver Charm was retired shortly thereafter.

Fear that the cardiopulmonary bleeding would create scar tissue in his lungs and perhaps prove fatal caused the Lewises to choose to retire the Charm to stud. He was too valuable to risk losing. In addition, he had performed admirably as a two-year-old, and spectacularly as a three- and four-year-old. Silver Charm had captivated crowds and cultivated fans wherever he went. There was certainly no shame in retiring as a five-year-old. He had earned a change in career.

CHAPTER 12

Sandy Hatfield

A work of art—

Before Aspen, Colorado became the favored destination for the rich and famous, a little girl named Sandy wandered the mountain-encircled pastures of her father's dude ranch. Guests came to experience the wilderness of the Colorado mountains, staying in the cabins and riding the horses. In the fall and even winter, her father became an outfitter and took hunters into the mountains to down their elk.

Life in the wilds of Colorado was perfect for her father, but not so for her mother. Before Sandy turned six, her parents divorced, sold the ranch, and moved back to Oklahoma, her mother to Oklahoma City, where she could enjoy the refined life, and her father to Ponca City, where he became a park ranger at Caw Lake.

So begins the backstory of another weaver of Silver Charm's tapestry.

Hatfield relished spending her summers with her father. It was with him that she could be with horses. Like Bob Baffert's and Gary Stevens' fathers, Hatfield's father got involved in Quarter Horse racing. Hatfield was just a young teen when she first became acquainted with life at the racetrack.

Upon graduating from high school, she went to Oklahoma State University in Stillwater. Hatfield lived with her older sister, Sarah Mussett. It was through her sister that she met a man named Jim Rudolph who was starting a horse program through the Animal Science Department at Murray State University in Kentucky. Hatfield was offered a full-ride scholarship, so she loaded up her Quarter Horse mare and moved to Murray to start her junior year in the Animal Science Department.

Her first exposure to the Thoroughbred industry came in the summer between her junior and senior years when she was offered a job working with the yearlings at Spendthrift Farm, a beautiful stallion farm in Lexington. Spendthrift was the home of large, white stables that were surrounded by lush green fields dotted with the dark bodies of grazing stallions. Several years later it also became known as the place where Seattle Slew first stood at stud before he was moved to Three Chimneys Farm. Working with the yearlings at such a famous farm was a dream job that Hatfield never wanted to wake up from. At the end of summer, Sandy Hatfield returned to Murray State for her senior year, but she rushed back to the Lexington area after graduation to work at Gainesway Farm. There she worked with the yearlings again. Her job with the yearlings included both groundwork and grooming to prepare the youngsters for the yearling sales.

Many years later, in 2008, the filly Winning Colors, which Gary Stevens rode to a Kentucky Derby victory, was buried on this farm. The threads of the tapestry continued to intertwine.

Sandy Hatfield's career began to expand as she was given new opportunities in the Thoroughbred industry. Hooper Roff, the manager of Crescent Farm introduced her to the breeding shed. In January of 1984, Hatfield moved to North Ridge Farm to work with Dan Elliott and Michael Osborne. She remained there for six years, the last two of which she was given her first opportunity to work as the stallion manager.

But the journey that led to her time working with Silver Charm had its challenges and heartaches. In July 1990, Hatfield entered the famous Calumet Farm through its elegant, red-painted gates to become the farm's broodmare manager. She worked at the farm from July 1990 to November 1991.

Calumet Farm was the birth and death place of the famous racehorse Alydar. Probably the greatest rivalry in Thoroughbred racing, and perhaps in all of sports, was the one between Affirmed and Alydar. The two battled alongside each other in all three of the Triple Crown races with a memorable duel down each home stretch. Affirmed went on to win each race, but Alydar is famous for coming in second in all three races. Affirmed and Alydar will forever be linked in the minds of horse racing devotees.

Alydar became a valuable stud, but on November 15, 1990, Alydar was euthanized as a result of a broken leg, having broken the same leg twice in two days. The initial break had occurred on November 13th. Several vets were called in. They decided to medicate the horse, apply a splint for the night, and try for surgery at the Calumet clinic in the morning. After the medication was administered and the splint applied, the champion horse laid down in the deep straw. With aching hearts, the resident vet, Dr. Linda Rhodes, and Sandy Hatfield, who was in charge of the broodmares at the time, spent the entire night sitting on the straw, holding and stroking Alydar's head.

Hopes were cautiously high after the surgery, but on the fifteenth, Alydar, fighting against the sling and cast, rebroke his leg in a new place. There was really no choice but to end his suffering. These many years later, it is still a painful subject for Hatfield to discuss.

In decline through the 1980's, Calumet Farm was forced into bankruptcy after the loss of Alydar. It would have ceased to exist if not for Henryk de Kwiatkowski, a Polish-born aeronautical engineer who made a fortune in business after moving to North America. Kwiatkowski bought Calumet Farm with a bid of $17 million less than an hour before it was to be auctioned as acreage for development in 1992. He died in 2003, but his restored Calumet Farm passed to his family members as a group of trustees.

In the wake of Alydar's death and the ensuing crisis, Hatfield applied for the job of Broodmare Manager at the stunningly beautiful Gainsborough Farm. To her surprise, she was offered the job of Stallion Manager. Beginning in January 1991, she became the first woman in the United States to manage the stallions at a major Thoroughbred breeding stable. She remained in that position for the next eight years.

One day in December 1999, Hatfield answered the phone in the Gainsborough Farm office. The person who greeted her through the line was a friend named Dan Rosenburg. He asked her if she knew of someone who would be interested in the job of Stallion Manager at Three Chimneys Farm. Headquartered in Midway, just outside Lexington, Three Chimneys has been home to several Kentucky Derby winners, including 1977 Triple Crown winner Seattle Slew, 1980 champion filly Genuine Risk, Smarty Jones (2004), Big Brown (2008) and . . . Silver Charm.

Now, Rosenburg was calling her about finding a new Stallion Manager! She responded, "What about me?"

"We can't afford you," he said.

But things have a way of working out. By the time Hatfield hung up the phone, a deal had been struck, and she had a new job.

Silver Charm had been at Three Chimneys since July and had not yet started his first breeding season. Hatfield was intrigued by the possibility of working with him. In January of 2000, Hatfield arrived at Three Chimneys Farm to take the position she would hold for the next twenty-five years.

It became her turn to add weft in Silver Charm's life.

CHAPTER 13

Living at Three Chimneys

Our legacy.

Everyone at Three Chimneys Farm was excited about the first day of Keeneland's summer yearling sale in July 1999—until something more exciting happened.

The Sunday before the first day of the sale, the staff at the farm learned the famous stallion, Silver Charm, would be joining Seattle Slew in their breeding program. As if that wasn't thrilling enough, the Charm was to arrive the very next day between 1:30 and 2:00 in the afternoon. That didn't give the farm staff much time to prepare a proper welcome.

Monday broke brightly, not a cloud in the sky to darken anyone's spirits. By 1:30 that afternoon,

Robert and Blythe Clay, the owners of Three Chimneys Farm; Bob and Beverly Lewis and their son and daughter-in-law; as well as many friends and staff joined news reporters to witness the famous gray stallion's arrival. His new career was about to begin.

The Stallion Barn. Silver Charm's stall at Three Chimneys was the one immediately to the right of the entrance. (Photo by the author.)

The excitement was palpable as the Sallee Horse Van pulled into the courtyard by the stallion barn. Everyone watched as the large ramp was lowered, hitting the ground with a deep sounding thud. The Charm, accompanied by Tom Wade, Seattle Slew's groom for the previous twenty years, appeared in the doorway. There, before everyone in attendance, stood a mature horse, a magnificent

Chapter 13 - Living at Three Chimneys

stallion at the peak of his powers. His nostrils were wide to absorb the unfamiliar odors. But he showed no other signs of anxiety as he walked elegantly down the ramp. The red crushed-rock walkway to the stallion barn became the Charm's red carpet. His fans lined the entire pathway, two and three people deep. The Lewises approached their horse to welcome him to his new home as pictures were taken.

Margaret Layton, the Communications and Marketing Director at Three Chimneys, wrote in her description of the event: "A turn or two later, Charm's sense of propriety had been satisfied, and he posed most cooperatively with Robert and Blythe Clay, and Bob and Beverly Lewis. When that duty was discharged, Tom and Charm made their way to the Stallion Barn, and to Charm's new home, in the stall closest to Seattle Slew's.

"We all crowded into the barn to see how he would react to his new surroundings. One question in people's minds was, *How would Seattle Slew react to the new kid?* Slew reacted as he often does, when not the center of attention, by turning his back and surveying his kingdom outside one of his two full-length doors. I almost laughed aloud a bit later when Charm unwittingly adopted the exact same stance when he momentarily tired of all the people looking at him!

"But overall, Charm continued to conduct himself with the utmost of courtesy and professionalism. I began to wonder if he had 'read the book' on how one would like a horse to act. When I expressed that sentiment to someone later, they said, 'No, he *wrote* the book!'"

Three weeks earlier, while Silver Charm was at Churchill Downs, the fans had been allowed to sign a 6- by 4-foot goodbye card. The card was brought to Three Chimneys for all in attendance to read the sentiments shared by his fans. People from all walks of life had recorded their memories of the thrills he had given them. The twenty-four races he had run, the $6,944,369 he had netted, and the heart-stopping photo finishes had all been embedded in so many people's remembrances of this dashing Thoroughbred and recorded on the giant card.

Sandy Hatfield with Silver Charm
(Photo from Hatfield, used with permission)

Six months later, in January 2000, Sandy Hatfield entered the elegant stallion barn at Three Chimneys, with its soaring cathedral ceiling

Chapter 13 - Living at Three Chimneys

supported by four giant arched wooden beams, as the new Stallion Manager. To her right was the large box stall that was home to Silver Charm and next to it, the stall that housed Seattle Slew. A huge responsibility now rested upon her shoulders. Breeding season was soon to be upon them and Hatfield needed to be ready.

Hatfield told me in an interview that she felt an immediate attraction to the famous horse, and soon learned to love and appreciate the idiosyncrasies that made Silver Charm everyone's favorite. She formed an instant connection with the big gray stallion. He was very easy to be around. He loved people, especially those who offered him treats. He was cooperative to work with. He could be led on a long rein while he pranced beside her. He exuded confidence.

Sandy Hatfield learned that Silver Charm didn't like being brushed. He would pin his ears and swing his head to the side, but never bite, when she brushed him to get him ready to show to a potential client.

I asked Hatfield in an interview what she thought of Seattle Slew. "He was a complete jerk!" she said.

The most difficult part of working with Silver Charm was teaching him how to breed with a mare. One would think it would come naturally, and for some horses it did. But Silver Charm had been conditioned to not be aggressive around other horses; it was hard for him to put that earlier training aside when in the breeding barn.

Gary Stevens told me in our interview that the

Charm was always kind to other horses on the racetrack. He said he could remember only one time when the Charm had been aggressive toward another horse. They were going down the track at Santa Anita toward the gates. Charm was acting unusually hot; he normally took everything in stride. But, for some reason, he was stirred up in the pre-race. After just eight minutes out on the track, Silver Charm reached over and bit the lead pony on the neck. Stevens was shocked. He said to the pony girl, "Either this will be really good or really bad." It turned out to be really good. Silver Charm won that race by six lengths, the most he had ever won by.

Sandy Hatfield said in our interview that it took a couple of weeks of careful guidance before the Charm became an effective stud.

At that time, the stallions were still ridden. Hatfield remembers watching the Charm's favorite rider, Brian, gallop him up and down the rolling hills on the farm. The Charm had a great relationship with this particular rider.

Silver Charm's fee was only $25,000. Considering his race career, that was low. However, his pedigree was not considered particularly strong. Bob Baffert once said in an article for *BloodHorse Magazine*: "He's bred just like Skip Away, by nothing out of nothing. Let's hope he ends up winning as much money (as Skip Away)." He didn't. He missed by $2.65 million.

During the years Silver Charm stood at stud at Three Chimneys, the Lewises and Bob Baffert came to visit him several times, and he always knew who

Chapter 13 - Living at Three Chimneys

they were. We have eventually learned that horses have a remarkable memory.

Silver Charm stood at stud for five years at Three Chimneys. Overall, his progeny won more than 1,000 races for over two million dollars in earnings. In 2004, the Lewises sold Silver Charm to a Japanese breeding conglomerate called Shizunai Stallion Station. Bob Lewis told the *Daily Racing Form*, "We received an offer that, at my stage of life, we could not turn down." With the exchange of funds, Silver Charm left his home and friends in the United States. He was loaded in the belly of a large jet and flown over the ocean to the island nation of Japan.

On August 6, 2007, Silver Charm was inducted into the National Museum of Racing and the Racing Hall of Fame. He was the second Hall of Fame horse for Bob and Beverly Lewis, the first being Serena's Song. At this time, Silver Charm was in Japan and was most likely not aware of this huge honor! Bob Baffert said of the honor: "Horses like him who have that something extra and show the courage he did are the kind of horses that get in the Hall of Fame."

Sadly, Bob Lewis didn't live to see Silver Charm given such high recognition. However, Beverly Lewis did, and she praised the horse this way: "He was special wherever he went, and you always felt good when you were around him. Everyone loved Silver Charm, and by going into the Hall of Fame, he's where he belongs."

After several years living in the northernmost reaches of Japan, Silver Charm's gray dapples faded and were replaced by brown freckles on a white coat. On a typical misty day, he appeared to be an apparition, symbolic of his popularity as a stud fading quickly. The Charm was not considered a very successful sire in Japan. His foals were not standouts on the track. Therefore, each year, fewer and fewer mares were brought to him. Even though he was a favorite with his Japanese grooms due to his kind nature, by the tenth year, he was not earning his keep, and he was going to be retired. Fortunately for all those who love him, the Lewises had put a clause in the sale contract so that they could get him back if the Japanese firm retired him from breeding.

This began the weaving of the next part of his life's tapestry.

Part 2
RETIREMENT

Old Friends Farm

When speed fades from the fire of their stride,
And the cheers of the crowd no longer rise,
We gather them close, with hearts open wide,
And lift them from the tracks' fading ties.

No more the whip, no more the race,
Just fields of green, a quiet place,
Where they can roam at their own pace,
Free from the bridle, free from the chase.

Their hooves no longer pound the dirt,
But still they carry lessons learned,
Of courage gained 'neath shirts of silk,
Of battles fought, and victories earned.

In quiet pastures, freed from the race,
They find their peace, they find their grace—
For every horse deserves a rest,
A life of love, where they are blessed

The True Horseman

As I did my research for this book, I encountered many men and women who I would define as true horsemen.

And at least one who didn't know he was, until time passed and horses had become his passion.

"What is a true horseman?" you might ask.

I gave that a lot of thought over the year I worked on this book, and I came up with one summary statement that I then broke down into several qualifiers.

My conclusion: A true horseman sees the horse as a partner, not a tool.

Let me expand.

A true horseman is not measured by the ribbons on his wall or the silver on his saddle.

He is measured in the quiet moments—in the way a wild-eyed colt settles at his touch, in the way an old mare leans into his hand, melting the years between them.

A true horseman knows the language of a flicked ear, a tightened flank, a heavy sigh, a lick and a chew.

He rides with feel, not force; he teaches with patience, not pride. He does this by listening more than he speaks—and then, when he must speak, the horse will listen.

To him, every horse is a world unto itself—not

something to be conquered, but something to be understood, honored. If he's lucky, he's invited into a partnership.

He knows that to lead a horse, you must first be worthy of being followed.

And so he learns, every day, again and again, from hooves and hearts far wiser than his own.

In the end, a true horseman leaves no trail of broken spirits behind him—only a legacy of horses who carry his kindness in their blood, long after he is gone.

For every racehorse, there comes a time when the cheering stops. That's when the real horsemen step in.

We all need someone at certain times in our lives to weave new colors into our tapestry. For Silver Charm, fate, or the hand of God brought him just the weavers he needed at just the right time—retirement.

Even legends need someone to lead them gently home.

CHAPTER 14

Ferdinand

When speed fades from the fire of their stride...
And the cheers of the crowd no longer rise...

Amid the rolling hills of the Clairborne Farm near Paris, Kentucky, a bright chestnut colt was born in a large stall covered in deep straw. It was March 12, 1983. Destined to be a great one, he was the son of England's last Triple Crown winner, Nijinsky II. His dam was Banja Luka, and he was the result of careful planning by his owners and breeders, William and Elizabeth Keck. They named him Ferdinand.

Elizabeth and her husband William owned the largest independent oil company in North America. In addition to investing in racehorses such as Ferdinand, they also invested in Indianapolis 500 race cars. The two were very generous with their money, donating to several universities. They even funded the design and construction of the Keck Telescope on the summit of Hawaii's dormant Mauna Kea volcano. A minor planet *5811 Keck* was named in their honor.

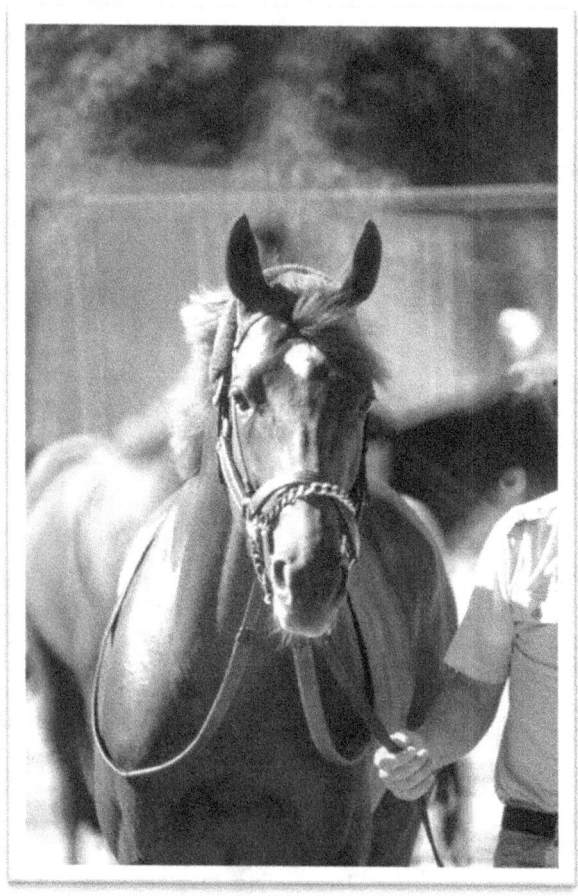

Ferdinand
(Keeneland Library Barrett Collection)

Ferdinand grew strong and beautiful and was soon put under the careful and patient supervision

Chapter 14 - Ferdinand

of trainer Charlie Whittingham. With famous jockey Bill Shoemaker on board, Ferdinand lived up to expectations. He won eight of twenty-nine starts and earned $3,777,978 during his racing career.

His record of accomplishments reads like a submission in the "Who's Who" of Thoroughbred racing. He won the 1986 Kentucky Derby and the 1987 Breeders' Cup Classic, just to name two. In 1987 he was honored to receive two Eclipse Awards, one for Horse of the Year, and the other for Champion Older Male.

In 1989, Ferdinand was retired to stud at the Claiborne Farm.

In 1994, the Keck's sold Ferdinand to Japan's JS Company to be used as a stud. Mrs. Keck, who was the owner of record, assumed that Ferdinand would be returned when he was no longer being used for breeding.

The stallion spent several years at the Arrow Stud Farm on the island of Hokkaido. His groom at the stud, Toshiharu Kaibazawa, told Barbara Bayer, a reporter for *BloodHorse* magazine, he was "the gentlest horse you could imagine. He'd come over when I called to him in the pasture. And anyone could have led him with just a halter on him...He'd come over to me and press his head up against me. He was so sweet."

In 2003, the Kecks inquired about bringing him back to the U.S. They received no response. Reporter Bayer undertook an investigation to learn Ferdinand's whereabouts. She discovered that Ferdinand was bred to just ten mares in his final year at the farm. As a result, the owners decided to get rid of him. They initially tried to place him at a riding stable, but when this failed, he was placed in the hands of a horse dealer named Yoshikazu Watanabe on February 3, 2001. No one had attempted to notify the Kecks or Claiborne Farm of these decisions.

When Bayer set about trying to find the horse, she was told several lies, including that Watanabe had given Ferdinand to a friend; that he had been gelded; and that he was at a riding club somewhere. The story about him being gelded was demonstrably false, as he was bred to six mares in 2001 and two more in 2002.

Despite Watanabe's many deceitful attempts to mislead Bayer as to Ferdinand's whereabouts, the reporter discovered that Ferdinand had been "disposed of" in late 2002. His Japanese registration was annulled on September 1, 2002.

Bayer wrote in her article for *BloodHorse*, "In Japan, the term 'disposed of' is used to mean slaughtered."

The heartbreaking news of Ferdinand's fate sent shockwaves through his admirers in the United States. For those who had cherished the Kentucky Derby champion, the realization that nothing—neither wealth nor influence, not even the Kecks' deep pockets—could change his tragic end was devastating. Yet, out of sorrow rose a powerful movement. His story ignited a fire in the hearts of many, compelling them to take action, ensuring that no other Thoroughbred would suffer the same cruel fate once its racing or breeding days were over.

Chapter 14 - Ferdinand

And, thus, Ferdinand became another weaver in Silver Charm's tapestry.

CHAPTER 15

Michael Blowen

*We gather them close, with hearts open wide,
And lift them from the tracks fading ties.*

Beginning at the age of twenty-eight, Boston native Michael Blowen was the movie critic for *The Boston Globe*. One Saturday afternoon while taking a break from the hustle and bustle of the city's largest newsroom—heads bent over computer screens, people rushing in and out and between desks as deadline nears—Blowen was relaxing at home. His phone rang. Reaching over to answer it, he recognized the voice of his editor at *The Globe*, Robert Taylor.

"Want to go to the racetrack?" Taylor asked. Blowen had never liked horse racing; in fact, whenever *Sports Illustrated* magazine put a horse on the cover, he would throw the issue away. But Taylor was his boss, after all, so he agreed to go.

Chapter 15 - Michael Blowen

The outing to Suffolk Downs that day became the first of many for Michael Blowen. He admitted during our interview that it wasn't the horses that initially fascinated him about horse racing—it was *The Daily Racing Form*! He became addicted to figuring out how to read it and interpret the numbers to actually make money from betting.

Eventually, however, he began to feel a connection to the horses themselves. The pounding hooves nearing the finish line sent vibrations deep into his soul.

He admits that initially he was afraid of horses. They were big and powerful, and some seemed a bit wild. However, on a cold February day in 1997, he attended the races at Suffolk Downs and placed a big bet on a horse he was sure would win him a lot of money. The horse won, all right, but the excitement was fleeting as a short time later the horse was disqualified.

He decided to walk off his crushing disappointment and found himself on the lower levels of the grounds. Fate, or the hand of God, was at work when he ran into Carlos Figueroa, a trainer he knew, having previously interviewed him for an article. After visiting for a while, Blowen asked the trainer if he could come work for him and learn about horses. And that is how it began—he would show up at the barn at 6 a.m. and work as a groom until 8:15. A subway ride would get him to *The Globe,* and he'd transform into a movie critic by 10 a.m.

He expected to learn about the care of horses while working for Figueroa. However, while there, he was exposed to a very troubling aspect of the horse racing industry. From time to time, a truck would show up at the grounds and take away a horse or two that was no longer racing—read that as "no longer making any money." The truck was there to take the horses "away." Blowen learned that "away" meant the horse would be taken to the slaughter. As the horses were being loaded, some of them would let out a heart-wrenching sound that could only be described as a scream. It was a sound that haunted him in his dreams. He firmly believed that the horses knew what was about to happen to them.

At the time, he was playing on a men's intramural basketball team. As the players got older, the team started to fall apart. So, Blowen came up with the idea to buy a racehorse jointly as a way to keep the team together. They purchased a horse named Fly McGrew. The horse never won a race. Michael Blowen laughed as he told me the story. Fly McGrew was retired and retrained to become a jumper.

Michael Blowen began working at *The Globe* in 1976. But in 2001, the paper was bought by the *New York Times*, and he and his wife, Diane White, who was also a columnist for the same paper, were offered buyouts. Now was the time to reevaluate what he wanted to do with his life.

Michael kept thinking about an article he had previously written for *The Globe* earlier that year about a horse named Saratoga Character, or 'Sara' for short. The article was published on March 1, 2001, and told the story of Sara, who had been injured while racing and was purchased by Kim Zito, wife of trainer Nick Zito. Kim then donated the

Chapter 15 - Michael Blowen

horse to the Thoroughbred Retirement Foundation, which sets up horse therapy programs in prisons. Sara was sent to the Blackburn Correctional Campus in Lexington, Kentucky. Michael told me, "The best day in Saratoga Character's life was the day he set foot in prison."

Michael considered what he had learned while writing the article and how impressed he was with the Thoroughbred Retirement Foundation (TRF), which is headquartered in Saratoga Springs, New York. Then, as fate, or the hand of God, would have it, he attended a fundraiser for the organization at Belmont Park. While talking with a group of people who were involved with the organization, the idea was thrown out that Blowen should be their Operations Director.

His initial response was negative. But the seed was planted, and he couldn't stop it from growing. Having lived his entire life in Boston, this would be a big change. His one son was out of the home. He was now a "recovering movie critic" and having seen it all, he never wanted to go to movies again. But horse racing was becoming a favorite pastime. So, it seemed a big change was just what he needed. TRF sweetened the pot by agreeing to let him work out of its Kentucky office—where Blowen wanted to be so that he was where the action was in the racing world.

Now there was just one more hurdle to overcome—his beloved wife Diane. He finally worked up the courage to propose the idea to her.

"How would you like to move to Kentucky?"

For twenty minutes, there was no response.

Then she said, "I'll go with you, but only on one condition."

"What's that?"

"That when I leave you, you won't try to follow me!"

A few days later, they were on their way to Kentucky and neither one has looked back! (She never left him!)

Work at TRF was rewarding. Michael had the opportunity to save many horses from slaughter. He attended sales and purchased horses that would otherwise have lost their lives. Most were injured and couldn't be used for racing or retrained to a new career. However, he discovered one problem. Most of the Thoroughbred Retirement programs and farms would not take stallions.

CHAPTER 16

The Birth of Old Friends Farm

No more the whip, no more the race,
Just fields of green, a quiet place,

As it became increasingly difficult to place stallions—they were harder to handle than mares or geldings and had to have their own paddock, which meant more space—Michael Blowen continued to mull the idea of starting a retirement farm for stallions. Eventually, the idea drove him to action. He soon even had a name for it...Old Friends.

Sure that everyone else in the industry would agree that it was a great idea, he started talking about it to people he thought would want to help. Rejection after rejection didn't stop him. With no one initially willing to help, he decided he would just do it himself! He was certain the idea could not fail.

After months of negative responses, discouragement was raising its ugly head. He went to visit a friend who owned a store in Midway, seeking a sympathetic ear. Picking up *The Daily Racing Form,* he stepped outside and sat on a bench. His entire body spoke of failure—head down, shoulders hunched, a sigh here and there.

Midway, Kentucky's first town founded by a railroad, is a charming little village known for being the home to several world-famous Thoroughbred breeding farms. Located close to Lexington, it is in the center of Bluegrass country. Even though it has a population of around only 3,000, its quaint architecture, especially along Railroad Street, attracts visitors to its restaurants and boutiques.

Such was the case on the day Blowen sat on a bench, deep in reflection and filled with discouragement. Fate, or the hand of God was at work once again. Betty Sue Walters, who was walking along the sidewalk, noticed his dejected look and stepped up. Blowen recounts the conversation in *History of Old Friends*:

"She asked me, 'What's the matter?' I explained my idea and how no one seemed to be interested in helping, and then added, 'Well, I've got some horses coming in, and I've got no place for them and everything else. There's no...'

And, she said, 'Well I've got a farm.'

I said, 'You do?'

She said, 'Yes. You want to come and look at it?'

I replied, 'Yeah!'

Chapter 16 - The Birth of Old Friends Farm

So that's the only reason we stayed in Kentucky. Because Betty Sue saw me sitting on a park bench moaning and groaning and acting like a big old baby and screaming out at the world, and she came by and said, 'Well, wait a minute, I've got a farm.' And that's how we ended up over at Afton Farm."

That February day in 2003 became a lot warmer in that moment.

The first horse he brought to Afton Farm was Invigorate, a gelding he had worked with earlier. This horse was followed by the movie star, Rich in Dallas, who was one of the horses that played the part of Seabiscuit in the movie.

The first official retiree at the Old Friends Farm, a home established for stallions, was actually a mare that had been deserted at a sale barn. Blowen felt her name, Narrow Escape, was fitting. Ironically, the mare's stud was Exceller, another hall of fame Thoroughbred who, like Ferdinand, was slaughtered overseas. The mare narrowly escaped the same fate. It is interesting to note that Exceller was the only horse to beat two Triple Crown winners in the same race, Seattle Slew and Affirmed.

But it was when Blowen read about the slaughter of Ferdinand that Old Friends' future changed. Learning about what befell the beloved Ferdinand pierced Blowen's heart and he feared for the other American horses living in Japan at the time. The article mentioned Sunshine Forever and Criminal Type, two champion stallions whose lives were at risk. Blowen knew both of these horses and had seen them run when they were in the U.S. He couldn't let them face the same end as Ferdinand, and if anyone was going to save them, it would have to be him.

Bringing a horse back from Japan is not an easy task. The first issue is the language barrier. It wasn't until he connected with an international horse dealer, Emmanuel de Seroux, that he was able to explain to the Japanese owners what he wanted to do. Seroux had sold the horses to the Japanese breeders in the first place and was able to communicate with them and convince the owners to release the horses.

The second major problem is that it is expensive to fly horses internationally. At the time, the price tag was $45,000, and for Old Friends Farm, running on a slim budget of donations, that figure seemed an insurmountable challenge. This problem was solved when Blowen's mother-in-law co-signed a loan that made up the difference between what people donated and what was needed.

Sadly, Criminal Type, the famous son of Alydar, did not live to see his homeland again.

The death of Criminal Type left an empty stall on the plane that was quickly filled by Creator, another champion Thoroughbred being retired.

The success of Blowen's efforts to bring these stallions home touched many people's hearts. More stallions were retired there and more donations flowed in. Old Friends became so well-established and respected that it wasn't long before a larger farm was needed. The hand of God was at work

Chapter 16 - The Birth of Old Friends Farm

again, this time in the form of Alfred Nuckols.

Nuckols owned a farm in Midway called Hurstland. On November 4, 2004, Sunshine Forever and Creator, made their way from Japan to New York, and finally to Hurstland Farm. But as Blowen continued to accept more horses, and not just stallions, he had to build more and more paddocks. As I mentioned earlier, each stallion needs to be in its own space, while the mares and geldings that Blowen couldn't turn away could be grouped together.

I might mention here that a bit of foreshadowing occurred when Bonnie's Poker, Silver Charm's mother, became one of the early mares brought to the farm. She arrived at the farm in December 2004, joining Narrow Escape. The two became fast friends.

At the same time, Nuckols was trying to run his own horse breeding and training business. Then something wonderful happened. From the movie *Field of Dreams* came the saying, "If you build it, they will come." This proved to be true for Old Friends at Hurstland. Tourists started coming. Horse lovers wanted to meet their heroes, and Michael Blowen loved showing them off. Nuckols enjoyed letting people see the horses, from new foals to retired champions. It was working well, and Old Friends' fame was spreading.

People who are unfamiliar with horses, or just getting their feet wet in the equine world, will appreciate Blowens' comments in "History of Old Friends."

"When we were at Hurstland Farm, I was a

real, real novice with horses. I don't know a lot now, but I knew even less then. I would panic over the littlest thing. A horse would get a little cut or something, and I'd go, 'Oh, should I call the vet?' And Alfred (Nuckols) would look at me like I was from outer space. And for good reason. He was an experienced horseman. He knew the difference between something that was not dangerous and not lethal and not terrible and something that was serious. You only called the vet when it was serious."

While Michael Blowen was grateful for Nuckols' willingness to share Hurstland with Old Friends, he began to set his sights on owning his own farm. He describes it this way in *History of Old Friends*:

"I used to have these nightmares of something happening at Hurstland Farm, and all of a sudden there is no place for these horses. I had this nightmare of all these stallions running down the middle of the street in Midway. It used to drive me nuts.

"So, I started to look around a little bit...then we saw Dream Chase Farm in Georgetown, and I knew it would be ideal because it was near the interstate, it was near the Kentucky Horse Park, it had easy access and would be very good for the visitors and there was a lot of room for the horses. There was already a lot of fence here, a house we could use for a bed and breakfast and a house we could use for the office."

Chapter 16 - The Birth of Old Friends Farm

This is the Old Friends Office that greets you when you arrive. (photo by the author)

The price tag of nearly two million dollars was not going to deter Blowen. He had a way of figuring out what he had to do to get what he wanted. At the recommendation of a friend, he went to visit Whitaker Bank, a locally owned bank in Georgetown. With his financial records in hand and promising to never miss a payment, he convinced the bank owner and the bank president to visit Old Friends at Hurstland. Two weeks later Old Friends had a beautiful new home.

CHAPTER 17

Returning home

*Where they can roam at their own pace,
Free from the bridle, free from the chase.*

After ten years as a stud in Japan, Silver Charm was to be retired. Case Clay at Three Chimneys had been keeping close contact with the Japanese breeders. As I mentioned previously, the Lewises loved Silver Charm so much that they had put a clause in their sale contract that said he would be returned to the United States at the Lewis' expense if he was no longer being used as a stud. This is called "The Ferdinand Clause." Beverly Lewis, her son Jeff, along with Clay at Three Chimney's Farm, worked out all the details. Bob Lewis was deceased by this time. On October 29, 2014, Three Chimneys Farm announced that Silver Charm would be returning to his homeland and would be

Chapter 17 - Returning home 109

permanently retired at Old Friends in Georgetown, Kentucky.

Silver Charm arrives at Old Friends Farm led by Sandy Hatfield-(Used with permission)

Sandy Hatfield, who, you will recall from Chapter Thirteen, oversaw Silver Charm when he was standing at stud at Three Chimney's Farm, was the one who had the opportunity to call Michael Blowen. "How would you like an old gray stallion?" she asked, her smile vibrating through the phone line.

Blowen had never met Silver Charm in person but had idolized him for some time. In fact, he named the Shetland pony at Old Friends, "Little Silver Charm," after the stallion. Sworn to secrecy, Michael was near to bursting. But he had to keep it quiet until the Lewises released the news to the press.

The *Paulick Report* released the following statement from the Lewis family:

"The Robert and Beverly Lewis family are thrilled and proud to have Silver Charm returning to America and beginning his retirement at Old Friends Equine in Georgetown, Kentucky. The racing thrills and excitement that he brought to our lives will never be forgotten. Winner of the 1997 Kentucky Derby and Preakness Stakes, the 1998 Dubai World Cup and numerous other graded stakes, Silver Charm demonstrated amazing heart and competitiveness during his four-year racing career. His 2007 induction into the Thoroughbred Racing Hall of Fame was proper recognition of his great career on the track.

We extend our gratitude to J.B. and Kevin McKathan, who spotted him as a two-year old in Florida, Bob Baffert, who so capably trained him, Gary Stevens, who rode him to his greatest victories, Rudy, his groom, who cared for Silver Charm wherever he went, Three Chimney's Robert

Chapter 17 - Returning home

Clay and Dan Rosenburg, who managed his U.S. stud career, the Japan BloodHorse Breeders Association, who managed his Japanese stud career, Case Clay, who was instrumental in assuring his return home, and Michael Blowen, who was steadfast in his determination to see Silver Charm, one day, residing at Old Friends.

We hope that thoroughbred racing fans from around the world will enjoy visiting Old Friends and saying "Hello" to one of America's great race horses!"

As mentioned earlier, bringing a horse back to the United States is a long and expensive venture. Silver Charm was first flown to Chicago where he was put in quarantine. He was picked up in a large horse transport van by Sallee Van Lines and brought to their facility in Lexington.

Sandy Hatfield spent a sleepless night on November 30th, filled with excitement of what the next day would bring. She had a surprise in the works. Knowing Silver Charm was arriving at the Sallee facility the next morning, she had arranged to meet him. She stood outside the large van as the doors were opened and the ramp lowered. Then he appeared and her heart fluttered.

Standing at the top of the ramp, nostrils flared and ears flicking, Silver Charm posed and surveyed his surroundings. She took his lead, led him down the ramp, and loaded him into a smaller trailer, one that could get onto the Old Friends property. She stayed in the trailer and rode with him the rest of the way to his new home.

It was December 1, 2014, a day both Sandy Hatfield and Michael Blowen remember well. The day of Silver Charm's arrival at Old Friends was cold and dreary. But that was not how one would describe the sparkling eyes and pounding hearts of Michael Blowen and the staff at the farm as they watched the trailer pull onto the property.

When the side door opened, Sandy stood in the doorway, her gray hair pulled back in her customary ponytail, framing her beaming face like a halo. An effulgent smile filled her face. Then a large, flea-bitten gray horse appeared beside her and a cheer went up from the small assemblage. Like a movie star on the red carpet, Silver Charm descended the ramp.

Sandy and Michael led him to the barn where he would be quarantined. All stallions must prove that they are not carrying CEM: Contagious Equine Metritis. CEM is a highly infectious bacterial disease of the reproductive tract in horses caused by bacterium that is spread during live cover breeding. The stallion must be bred to two mares who have been previously tested and found to be clean. After the breeding takes place, the mares are tested again and if they are still clean, all is well. The stallion, meanwhile, must remain in quarantine until the results come back proving that he is not a carrier.

Chapter 17 - Returning home

Sandy Hatfield leading Silver Charm (Photo from Hatfield, used with permission)

A few days later, a "Welcome Home" party was held at Old Friends Farm for Silver Charm. It was a cold December day, but dozens of people came to the farm to see their hero. Sandy Hatfield led him out of the quarantine barn. The object of so much adoration was dressed in a warm, plaid Baker blanket. Hatfield paraded him around the paddock as camera's flashed. With head up and eyes sparkling, the Charm let everyone know he was back where he belonged!

When Gary Stevens heard that Silver Charm was back in the U.S. and in the quarantine barn at Old Friends Farm, he made arrangements to visit him. Stevens went to the farm after the stallion was released from quarantine, hoping for some private time with the horse he loved so much. Unfortunately, the press got word of his visit, and the sacred time alone was not to be during that first reunion. But the joy at seeing Silver Charm again overpowered any disappointment. The current of affection and trust that flowed between the horse and his jockey was palpable and beautifully captured in this photo taken by Matt Wooley, the famous equine photographer.

Silver Charm is welcomed back to the U.S. by Gary Stevens upon his arrival at Old Friends (Photo by Matt Wooley All rights reserved.)

Chapter 17 - Returning home

The October day I toured Old Friends Farm was perfect. The sky was a bright azure. The leaves on the trees that lined the driveway were just starting to turn red. There wasn't the slightest breeze to rustle them. The black, wooden fences (Blowen said the black paint lasted longer than the white) lined both sides of the drive as I sat beside my guide in the golf cart. Horses grazed in the pastures, the autumn sun warming their backs. As we rolled along, Michael Blowen began to spin a tale like yarn from a spindle, introducing me to the residents with the story of each horse's greatest feats. We passed the new Visitor's Center that had once been a tobacco barn. We passed the quarantine barn and paddock where a new arrival was being housed. And we passed the cemetery where Bonnie's Poker, Silver Charm's dam, is buried.

The rolling hills upon which the farm sat hid Silver Charm from my view until we reached the Blowen home. Across the lane, a white horse grazed at the far end of his paddock, unfettered as he shuffled across the rich green grass. Blowen stopped the cart, stepped out and grabbed a bucket of grated carrots from behind his seat. "He only has four teeth left," he explained.

The apple that I brought would have to remain in my bag.

At the sound of Blowen calling his name, the Charm lifted his head and pricked his ears. At thirty years of age, he refrained from galloping to the fence. He came toward us at a leisurely pace, sure that we would wait for him. "We let the horses do what they want. Their time of being told what to do every minute is over," Blowen told me.

When the Charm arrived at the fence, he lifted his head and nuzzled Blowen. Raising his head again, he knocked the bill of the golf cap with the Old Friends logo that Blowen wore. He was still a horse that loved people. Blowen's face beamed with affection, and he gave him some grated carrots.

I stepped up to the fence and got a kiss from Silver Charm as well. He stayed beside us as we talked; I'm sure he was well aware that we were talking about him. I noticed that, by thirty, he was showing the signs of old age. His coat is nearly all white. The gray dapples have been replaced by little brown freckles, making him what horsemen called "flea-bitten." His top line sagged a bit. His tongue lolled out of his mouth. But there was a proud sparkle in his eyes that could not be missed.

At this writing, Silver Charm has lived the life of a celebrity at Old Friends for more than ten years. As the oldest living Kentucky Derby winner, he is still an ambassador. He represents all the racehorses who once thrilled the crowds with their pounding hooves and flying manes as they reached for the finish line. A few of them became famous, most did not. But they all ran with their hearts full of desire. Now horse lovers from all over the world come to visit Silver Charm and the other gallant Thoroughbreds at Old Friends Farm in Georgetown, Kentucky.

A feeling of peace settles over each visitor as they watch the horses grazing in the fields. Many of these horses were the very ones they had cheered

Chapter 17 - Returning home 117

for in years gone by. But now, to reiterate the words of Michael Blowen, the blacks, bays, chestnuts and grays get to enjoy their well-earned rest and "...do whatever they want. Their time of being told what to do is over."

Silver Charm getting a kiss from Michael Blowen.
(Photo by the author)

Part 3
LEGACY

A Second Chance

Beneath the sun, a thunderous stride,
A thoroughbred's grace, once wild with pride.
Now weary limbs, no longer race,
Seek refuge in a quiet place.

Rescue hands reach, so firm, so kind,
To heal the wounds, both body and mind.
Each gallop slow, a battle won,
A new life starts beneath the sun.

The barns are filled with dreams reborn,
From tracks of dust to fields of morn.
Where hooves once beat in frantic haste,
Now calm and peace the past replaced.

For every horse whose race is done,
Rescue brings hope, a rising sun.
Through tireless work, they find their way,
A second chance, a brighter day.

Saving the Thoroughbreds

For many years, the story of a racehorse's life was a sad one. Most of them were viewed as a commodity whose sole purpose was to make money for their owners. If they couldn't make money on the racetrack, they were of little value for breeding. Therefore, they had to be disposed of. The lucky ones found new homes with loving families which used them for riding horses. Or they found new jobs as trail horses, jumpers, or dressage horses. A few even became therapy horses. While growing up in Oregon, I had several friends who bought "Off-Track Thoroughbreds"—OTTB's, as they were and still are called. But the number sold to happy homes was few compared to the large number born each year. That is starting to change.

The Jockey Club keeps records of the Thoroughbred foals born and, while the number has dropped in the last quarter-century, there are still more than 17,000 foals born each year. The majority of these horses are used for racing, at least for a time, but most horses are done racing by the age of five. That means they can have up to twenty-five years of life left during which they can bring love and joy to a new human family.

But for many horses, the slaughterhouse was the last thing they would see.

The racehorses at most risk of being slaughtered are those in the lower levels of the racing world. Remember, it was the famous horse,

Ferdinand, whose slaughter caused such an uproar. Many other racehorses died without anyone noticing. When I use the term "slaughter," I am not referring to the humane euthanasia of a sick or injured horse. While euthanasia is defined as a gentle, painless death provided to prevent suffering, slaughter is a brutal and terrifying end for horses.

Since 2007, it has been illegal to slaughter horses in the U.S. for human consumption. At that time, the last USDA slaughterhouses for horses, two in Texas and one in Illinois, were permanently shut down. However, thousands of horses are still being shipped to slaughterhouses in Canada and Mexico in deplorable conditions, with no food or water. The American Society for the Prevention of Cruelty to Animals (ASPCA) estimates that over 20,000 horses were transported over our borders in 2023 alone. I don't want to upset you with the horrific details of what the horses go through, both during transport and once they reach the slaughterhouse. You can look it up if you want, but you won't be happy with what you learn.

The meat the slaughterhouses harvest is shipped overseas to the many countries where horse meat is eaten. But it is important to note that the European Union passed a law in 2015 banning horse meat from Mexico because of the high level of toxins in the horse meat that Mexico provides. Unlike in Japan and Europe, the horses in the U.S. are not bred or raised for human consumption. We give them numerous medications that are carcinogenic or toxic for humans if consumed. These remain in the meat and can be passed on to

Chapter 17 - Returning home

humans when eaten.

In order to stop the inhumane transportation of horses out of the country with the intent to send them to slaughterhouses, a bill was proposed in Congress in 2023. Specifically, this bill, called the SAFE Act, HR 3475, prohibits a person from knowingly:

"slaughtering an equine for human consumption; or

shipping, transporting, possessing, purchasing, selling, or donating an equine to be slaughtered for human consumption or equine parts for human consumption." (from Congress.gov)

Congress, in 2024, passed the bill out of committee. However, as of this writing, the full Congress has not passed this bill and made it a law. If passed, the law would apply only in the United States.

Thanks to the efforts of so many horse-loving people, several organizations have been created to rescue the Thoroughbreds, and horses of all breeds, famous or not. Old Friends Farm is just one of those wonderful organizations. In the chapters that follow, I will tell you about a few of the other groups that are working tirelessly to save the Thoroughbreds.

CHAPTER 18

John Hettinger

Beneath the sun, a thunderous stride,
A thoroughbred's grace, once wild with pride.
Now weary eyes, no longer race,
Seek refuge in a safer place.

"All of my best friends have four legs," said John Hettinger. He is considered the father of thoroughbred rescue—the one person who raised the alarm louder than anyone else.

John Hettinger was born on December 18, 1933. He attended Yale University and earned his degree in American History in 1955.

Hettinger was fascinated by the history and culture of Mexico, so he went to work for a chemical company and lived and worked in Mexico City for eight years. After he and his wife, Betty, took a vacation to Spain, they decided to move there. While in Spain, he built a neighborhood of vacation homes near the Rock of Gibraltar. He sold this development to an investment bank for a large profit. In 1973, after seventeen years abroad, he and his wife, along with their two sons, James and William, decided it was time to return to the U.S.

The Hettingers took over Akindale Farm, with its 18th century house and fifty-five acres, from John's parents. Located in Pawling, New York, the farm was a beautiful example of New England acreage, with its rolling hills and numerous copses of deciduous trees whose leaves turned red in autumn. By purchasing neighboring properties, Hettinger expanded the farm to 500 acres. He set up a Thoroughbred breeding farm that became one of the premier operations in the U.S. Of all the successful horses that he bred, his favorite was a dark bay mare named Warfie, born on March 23, 1986.

Hettinger became an avid protector of horses, being concerned with preventing both their mistreatment and slaughter. He founded Blue Horse Charities in 2001 to that end and was involved in stopping the slaughter of horses in the U.S. Blue Horse Charities has helped support numerous horse rescue and retirement farms through the grants it awards. The ultimate goal of Blue Horse Charities is to keep the horses out of the hands of the "kill-buyers," as the Blue Horse Charities website states.

Hettinger was driven by the goal of ensuring every racehorse had a proper retirement after its racing career was over. To this end, in 2006, two

Chapter 18 - John Hettinger

years before his passing, he turned Akindale Farm into a beautiful sanctuary for retired thoroughbreds. It was initially started as a retraining and adoption program but eventually evolved into a retirement farm like Old Friends. At this writing, 103 retired racehorses call Akindale their home. A dedicated team, many of whom are volunteers, takes care of two herds of geldings and two herds of mares.

The current director of Akindale, Monique Coston said in an article for the *Paulick Report*, "Any horse that was bred by Akindale is always welcome to come back."

Hettinger was presented with the Eclipse Award of Merit in 2000. He was posthumously inducted into the Racing Hall of Fame in 2019. When he died in 2008, he left a legacy through his charities and his farm that will save Thoroughbreds for generations to come

CHAPTER 19

Thoroughbred Aftercare Alliance

Rescue hands reach, so firm, so kind,
To heal the wounds, both body and mind.
Each gallop slow, a battle won,
A new life starts beneath the sun.

Aftercare programs for the racehorses have exploded in recent years thanks in large part to Thoroughbred Aftercare Alliance. What happens to the racehorses when they are done racing or breeding is no longer the industry's dirty little secret, as Michael Blowen said to me. Now, many wonderful organizations are working to save the Thoroughbreds.

Chapter 19 - Thoroughbred Aftercare Alliance

"The Thoroughbred Aftercare Alliance has brought many aftercare organizations together with their creative fundraising, stringent requirements and, most of all, their love for our great athletes. They are directly responsible for Old Friends' increase in the number of retirees that we care for and, once they get here, the quality of care they receive. We can't thank them enough."
—Michael Blowen

Akindale and Old Friends are just two of the eighty-three organizations currently accredited by the Thoroughbred Aftercare Alliance (TAA). See the Appendix for the complete list. TAA is an organization that certifies a charity whose purpose is to care for retired Thoroughbreds. They evaluate the organization in five categories: operations; education; horse health care management; facility standards and services; and adoption policies and protocols. They provide help in the form of training and grants.

Their purpose is stated on their website:

"Funded initially by seed money from Breeders' Cup Ltd., The Jockey Club, and Keeneland Association Inc., Thoroughbred Aftercare Alliance is supported by owners, trainers, breeders, racetracks, aftercare professionals, and other industry groups.
"Since 2012, Thoroughbred Aftercare Alliance has granted more than $36.04 million to

accredited aftercare organizations and 18,500 Thoroughbreds have been retrained, rehomed, or retired by accredited organizations."

I am sharing three of those organizations with you on the following pages. Each one has taken a different approach to Thoroughbred aftercare, and each contributes to saving the Thoroughbreds in their own way.

New Stride Thoroughbred Adoption Society

On a cloudy day in March 2025, I left my hotel in British Columbia. As my husband Tom and I drove the thirty minutes to Langley, B.C., Canada, the rain turned to mist, so typical of the Pacific Northwest where I grew up. The rural town near the U.S./Canada border is home to New Stride Thoroughbred Adoption Society, an accredited TAA affiliate. I was eager to interview Carmen Forshaw, the organization's program coordinator and only paid staff person. We wove through narrow roads as overhanging trees dripped the last of the rainfall, arriving at the farm just in time for my 10:00 am appointment.

New Stride is housed at a hunter/jumper facility named Villa Training. One of the barns and several paddocks are set aside for the Thoroughbreds being cared for by New Stride. I found Forshaw in the covered arena, working with a bay mare whose registered name is Sweet as Honey. The horse was trotting in a large circle on a lunge line and displayed an uneven gate. As I talked with Carmen about the way she moved, she told me

Chapter 19 - Thoroughbred Aftercare Alliance

Honey came to them with a broken knee that has since healed and causes her no pain. But Honey would never be able to be much beyond a companion horse. Very light riding might be possible at best. We walked Honey to a paddock covered in deep mulch, put a blanket on her, then went into the barn for an interview.

Carmen Forshaw with Gwen, another resident of New Stride (Photo by the author)

New Stride was founded by a group of Backstretch People—the name given to the people who are credited with doing the actual care of the racehorses at a track—from Hastings Racecourse in Vancouver, B.C. The trainers, owners, grooms, and exercise riders from Hastings wanted to find a happy home for retired racehorses. As such, New Stride began as a retirement society. The founding members were Meril Agrey, Carol Anderson, Nancy Betts, Jim Boyes, John Knighton, Judy Knighton, Daniel Piotrowski, and Catherine Sheppard.

All the horses are donated by Hastings. Their ages range from as young as three to as old as eleven. The average age is five. Each has been used for racing during the previous season.

Over the years, New Stride has changed its focus. Its revised mission statement is: *Dedicated to finding adoptive homes and new careers for former Thoroughbred racehorses.* The facility takes up to seven horses at a time for retraining. Forshaw is the only trainer and usually works with each horse for about ten months before it is adopted. That, of course, varies with each horse. Their beautiful faces appear on the New Stride website, and status updates are frequent as the horses are prepared for adoption. The adoption fee is $1500—cheap for a horse these days. (Even my husband said, "How many are we taking home?") But we all know that the expense of owning a horse is much more than the purchase price! In fact, the adoption fee doesn't come close to the expense incurred by New Stride to care for and train the horse for several months or longer. As a result, the organization is very grateful for help it receives

Chapter 19 - Thoroughbred Aftercare Alliance

from TAA, as well as fund-raising efforts by its volunteer board and donations from Hastings Racecourse and many private donors.

Volunteers do the stall and barn cleaning and the feeding. Forshaw does most of the training and also works with some volunteers on groundwork. She teaches the volunteers how to work with the horses literally from the ground up. She mentioned that the racehorses come to her not even knowing how to be led beside a person. And they have only about a ten-to-fifteen-minute window that they are accustomed to being worked with. She uses the Dr. Andrew McLean Method and Natural Horsemanship theory, and teaches this to her volunteers.

During the several months that Forshaw has each horse, she moves the horse through groundwork exercises until she is eventually riding, if the horse is sound enough. When the horse does well at the walk, trot, and picking up a calm canter, she puts it up for adoption.

The adoption process begins with the completion of a detailed application. From this, Forshaw determines if the horse would be a good fit for the prospective buyer. She prefers to do a home visit if that is possible. Her goal is to place the horse in a home where both the horse and the owner can be successful.

The Thoroughbreds from New Stride have gone on to become everything from companion horses to trail horses to show horses in jumping, dressage and pleasure. This illustrates the talent and versatility of the breed.

Center for Racehorse Retraining

It was a surprisingly calm spring day in Wyoming when my husband Tom and I drove thirty minutes north of Cheyenne to a tiny rural town called Chugwater, population: 171 hardy souls. Southern Wyoming is known for its strong and irritating winds, often gusting up to ninety-miles per hour. But, today we were given a reprieve.

We exited I-25, drove under the freeway, and headed west. The prairie grasses, though sparse, were just awakening. Antelope and coyotes watched us pass, only mildly curious, as we disturbed the silence. White rock cliffs and barren plateaus surrounded us in every direction. No other cars joined us on the lonely country road as we made our way to our destination: Center for Racehorse Retraining (CRR).

Going through the gate and across the cattle guard, it wasn't long before we were greeted by several horses, still displaying their long winter

CRR official photograph. (Used with permission.)

Chapter 19 - Thoroughbred Aftercare Alliance

coats. I watched them move across the prairie, unencumbered by blankets or halters. "I feel like we are driving through a band of wild mustangs," I told Tom.

Little did I know, I was pretty close to being correct.

Driving up and over a ridge brought us in sight of two lovely homes, an enormous garage, and an even larger indoor arena. More horses roamed freely while several others were confined in large paddocks, lazily munching on hay.

Kate Anderson, Olivia Murray, and Tori Donovan greeted us with smiles on their faces as we pulled up to the arena. At the beginning of the interview, I learned that Kate is the founder and executive director of CRR, Olivia is the marketing director and media specialist, and Tori is the farm manager.

In 2016, Center for Racehorse Retraining was founded by Kate Anderson. By that time, Anderson had already amassed a long history of working with horses. She was trained in classical dressage both in the U.S. and in Europe. She was showing and teaching in the Rocky Mountain region.

Through a series of unexpected and even unplanned events, Kate and her family acquired some thoroughbred stallions and entered into the breeding business. She bred Thoroughbreds and Quarter Horses for ten years and became the "go-to" place for foaling in southern Wyoming. During that time, they were able to purchase the 2,500-acre ranch that I was now visiting.

The Andersons began using Kate's dressage

skills to retrain and rehome off-the-track Thoroughbreds. Kate's initial goal with the horses that came to CRR was to help them avoid retirement, but she soon found that many of the horses would probably not go on to new careers—their injuries were too severe. So, she turned those horses out on the ranch.

Then something surprising happened. Many of the horses she thought were a lost cause began improving. She began to see unexpected and unprecedented changes in their bodies, especially with regard to foot injuries.

She began intensive research into why this would be.

The horses turned out on the ranch became semi-feral. They learned to live like the wild mustangs. They were constantly on the move as they foraged. With the nearly constant movement, blood flow increased. With the increased blood flow, bone growth began and the feet began to repair themselves.

This discovery changed her whole approach to Thoroughbred aftercare, and people began to take notice. Racehorse owners from California and Kentucky began sending their horses to Anderson when their racing careers were over.

When a horse arrived at her ranch, the first thing Anderson did was remove its shoes, take it off grain, and turn them out on the prairie. The new horse, whether a mare or a gelding, would pick its own herd, (with mustangs in the wild this would be called "bands") and begin living a life it had never known.

Chapter 19 - Thoroughbred Aftercare Alliance

Anderson said she "let them return to being a horse."

The length of time the horse was given a "let-down period," as Anderson calls it, varied from three months to six years.

As one might expect, the horses went through an adjustment period. The shiny, muscled racehorse that first arrived at CRR soon began looking shaggy, sloppy and unkempt. But eventually, a transformation occurred. New muscle groups developed, and injuries, both physical and mental, began to heal. Even attitudes changed, and horses that had been difficult to handle previously became mild and cooperative.

Kate Anderson (left) and Olivia Murray
(Photo by the author.)

Kate Anderson's research has gained international attention. Careful records of foot repair and bone growth are kept through frequent radiographs. During our interview she showed me some of the digital pictures from the radiographs, enthusiastically pointing out the new bone growth in the hoof.

Help with her work has come from numerous sources, including Dr. Robert Bowker, a retired professor from Michigan State who has been researching foot issues. She also works with the Colorado State veterinary school's podiatry department. A local vet comes every week to take the radiographs that are so vital to tracking progress.

At the time of our interview, CRR was home to sixty-nine horses, eighty percent of which are Thoroughbreds. Five of the Thoroughbreds are products of her own breeding program, and the rest have been sent to her by their owners.

Since CRR's founding, upwards of two thousand horses have passed through the ranch or been permanently retired there. Many horses have gone on to be adopted, mostly to become family horses, trail horses, and even a few show horses. At the time of this writing, Center for Racehorse Retraining is the only place in the world that is running feral Thoroughbreds!

One horse that I met on the ranch, one that will never leave, was named Tina. The little mare is the daughter of the famous Thoroughbred stallion, Curlin, American Horse of the Year in both 2007 and 2008. Hopes for the mare were dashed when it was discovered that she was born with Turner

Chapter 19 - Thoroughbred Aftercare Alliance

Syndrome. This rare condition is the result of a missing X chromosome and can also appear in humans.

As a filly, Tina was undersized and crooked. Her owner did all that he could to help the little horse, which involved several surgeries to correct her physical deformities. But it was obvious that she would never be a racehorse. Out of a desire to do what would be best for the little horse, her breeder sent her to Kate Anderson at CRR. The breeder continues to be a generous donor to the Center for Racehorse Retraining, which speaks highly of the quality of people in the racing industry.

Harmony and Hope Horse Haven

More than seven decades ago, a brave little three-year-old girl climbed up on a fence that surrounded a small pasture in New Hampshire. Next to the fence, a large, shaggy draft horse dozed in the sun. Fearlessly, the child slipped off the fence and onto the old horse's broad back. Startled, the horse jerked up its head. His ears pinned back as he looked around to see who or what had interrupted his erstwhile pleasant day. It didn't take too many strides for the old horse to unseat his uninvited guest.

Such was the first time that Ruth Plenty ever rode a horse—and it ended with a spanking from her mother!

Many years later, when Plenty was in her early twenties, she was able to rescue a mare, one of several that had been in a terrible traffic accident in which the horse trailer carrying the horses was overturned. She paid just $97.50 for her and willingly took on the process of nursing the mare back to health. That was the first of many horses that Plenty would own throughout her life.

It was in 1994 that Plenty first fell in love with Thoroughbreds. She went on a tour of the Kentucky Horse Park and met a retired racehorse named John Henry, along with the Hall of Champion's barn manager, Cathy Robie. Her heart went out to the beautiful gelding, and she went back to visit him every day for the next week. She said those were the greatest seven days of her life. She left Kentucky with a tear in her eye and a love for Thoroughbreds in her heart.

Ruth Plenty had met her husband, Dennis White, in 1992. Her new husband was a racehorse enthusiast. In 1996, she was able to get a Thoroughbred of her own. The horse was a registered, unnamed mare who Plenty named Lady Maria. A hock injury kept the mare from racing, but she was bred and gave Plenty a beautiful filly.

The next horse Plenty acquired was Harmony, another mare off the track that was going through a year-long rest and recovery period. Harmony was then used as a broodmare, as well, and delivered a lovely colt.

While breeding Thoroughbreds was rewarding for Ruth Plenty, horse racing was not what appealed to her. She developed a passion for saving Thoroughbreds, not racing them. Her involvement in breeding racehorses was replaced by efforts to retrain retired horses. But the more she was around

Chapter 19 - Thoroughbred Aftercare Alliance

the racing world, the more she witnessed injury after injury. Far too many of the horses she observed could never be rehabilitated and go on to find successful new careers. Her heart was filled with compassion for these elegant animals which many viewed as worthless. And thus, Harmony and Hope Horse Haven was born.

In 2005, Harmony and Hope Horse Haven moved to a small farm in a town called New River, north of Phoenix, Arizona. As Phoenix expanded, it became necessary to find a more adequate place to call home. As a result, Harmony and Hope moved to Portal, Arizona on a forty-acre parcel of land two-and-a-half hours east of Tucson. What had once been high desert acreage, populated by cacti and sagebrush, became the home for dozens of rescued horses.

From 1996 with the rescue of Lady Maria and Harmony, until the present at this writing (2025), Harmony and Hope Horse Haven has provided a loving home and safe haven to ninety-two horses. In addition to the Thoroughbreds, Ruth Plenty has taken in a very petite Peruvian Paso Fino, a Missouri Fox Trotter, two Appaloosas, a Standardbred, a Friesian, several Quarter Horses, and five Standard Donkeys. At the time of this writing, Harmony and Hope is the home to fifty-one equines. Two mini donkeys and one mini horse join the forty-eight horses. Twenty-seven of the horses are Thoroughbreds.

The horses Plenty provides a home for are those with limited options. They require full retirement. Their injuries or limitations can be very restricting. But while their quality of life is a struggle, they can still get around well enough to preclude being euthanized. These are the horses that she wants to care for until their dying day.

F.W. Pirate with Ruth Plenty
(From Ruth Plenty-used with permission)

The horses at Harmony and Hope have come from various sources and places—from Oregon, California, Arizona, Utah and Kentucky. Plenty and her husband have purchased many of the horses themselves. Seventy percent of them arrive having been brought to them by former owners, track trainers, or placement organizations. One Quarter Horse by the name of "Hank," who had been a pony

Chapter 19 - Thoroughbred Aftercare Alliance

horse at the racetrack, was found at a feed lot. Their ages upon arrival typically range from four to twelve years old.

Many of the horses live quite long lives after arriving at Harmony and Hope. One example would be a particular mare who Ruth Plenty describes as "very feisty, and thought she ran the place." The mare lived to forty-one. Several of the horses she and her husband care for currently are in their late-twenties and thirties.

Each of the horses is in its own forty-five-by-sixty-foot paddock. Plenty has learned that keeping horses separated from one another cuts down on injuries and thus vet bills.

For the first twelve years of operation, Ruth and her husband Dennis funded Harmony and Hope entirely on their own, creating a place where horses could live out the rest of their lives in comfort, the same mission held by Old Friends Farm. However, caring for so many horses, many of whom need medical care, is a very expensive endeavor, one they could not continue to cover themselves.

Support has come in many forms. They have appreciated the help of the Thompson family, owners of Stronghold Feeds in Wilcox, Arizona. For twenty years (and counting), a flatbed truck, stacked high with two hundred and sixty bales of hay and 10,000 pounds of grains, pellets, and supplements has arrived at the farm. In addition to making their deliveries right on time, the Thompsons' sons even donate their time unloading and filling grain bins themselves!

But paying for feed and veterinary care has required additional help. Harmony and Hope received its first grant to help with the care of off-track Thoroughbreds from Thoroughbred Charities of America in 2010. Since 2013, Ruth and her husband have received a generous grant from the California Racehorse Management Account (CARMA) that I write about in the next chapter. In 2014, Harmony and Hope Horse Haven was accredited by TAA and received grants from that organization, as well. Other donations have come from former owners, people who followed a horse during its racing career, concerned individuals who just love horses, and private foundations.

Through the many and varied efforts from organizations like New Stride, Center for Racehorse Retraining, and Harmony and Hope Horse Haven, retired racehorses are finding either new careers or a new retirement home. But the people who care for these horses couldn't do what they do without the help of organizations like the Thoroughbred Aftercare Alliance and the California Retirement Management Account.

CHAPTER 20

California Retirement Management Account

The barns are filled with dreams reborn,
From tracks of dust to fields of morn.
Where hooves once beat in frantic haste,
Now calm and peace the past replaced.

Can a single woman trying to save a single horse really make a difference? That answer is a resounding, "Yes!"

Another old friend who is saving the Thoroughbreds is Madeline Auerbach. This impressive woman was born in Yorkshire, England in 1944. Her parents brought her to the United States when she was a small child. But this child was born with a love for horses. She was introduced to Thoroughbred racing by her late husband, Jim. After marriage, and starting a family which grew to three children, Patrick, Erin, and Harris, the Auerbach's made the leap into horse ownership. In

1977 they purchased a Thoroughbred racehorse named "Bravo Bravo." They continued to be involved in racing in California but on a small scale until they made the decision to buy a claiming horse for $80,000. That horse was Unusual Heat, and he changed their lives forever.

Unusual Heat didn't help them much on the track. He lost the only two races he ran under their ownership. But he had an amazing pedigree and a magnificent appearance. The Auerbachs retired him from racing after the 1996 season and started promoting him as a sire in 1998. In all, Unusual Heat sired 822 foals and lived to be twenty-seven, passing away in 2017. According to *BloodHorse* magazine, Unusual Heat was the all-time leading California sire for progeny earnings in 2008 and followed that up with eight consecutive years being the leading sire in California.

Arising from Unusual Heat's first crop of offspring was a colt named Lennyfromalibu. This colt was so stunning on the track that he brought recognition to his sire, and Unusual Heat's stud career blossomed. The Auerbach's became familiar figures in the California racing world, and their stable of horses began to grow. With the passing of her husband Jim in 2000, Madeline found herself responsible for the management of their business. Thus, in 2005, when it was time to retire Lenny, Auerbach was faced with a quandary: What to do with Lenny?

Auerbach began researching the options and came up dry. She discovered that the wealthy owners had large farms on which they could retire their horses. But most owners were not in a

Chapter 20 - California Retirement Management Account

position to do that. She was shocked to discover that there were extremely few options for horses such as Lenny, who could no longer race.

At that time, Auerbach was a director of the Thoroughbred Owners of California. In that capacity she started pushing the conversation about retirement options. She found that the majority of the owners were as concerned as she was. With Auerbach as the catalyst, several owners worked together to come up with the idea of creating the California Retirement Management Account or CARMA.

The mission statement on CARMA's website is straightforward:

The California Retirement Management Account (CARMA) provides funding for retirement of California-raced Thoroughbred horses and serves as an educational resource for the public and racing community.

The organizers came up with the idea to fund the account by asking the owners, trainers, and jockeys to contribute 0.03% of their winning purses to the account. It is set up as a voluntary commitment. In 2025, eighty percent of owners, trainers, and jockeys have chosen to participate, which I think speaks highly of them and their concern for the horses.

Lucinda Lovitt, now the Executive Director of CARMA, has had a long history with horses. Born and reared in Tucson, Arizona, Lovitt began riding English disciplines as a young child, competing in dressage, three-day eventing, and hunter/jumpers through her college years. It was while she was attending the University of Arizona that she was introduced to the horse racing world. U of A has a *Racetrack Industry* program, and a fellow competitor, Wendy Davis, was the director. With Davis's prompting, Lovitt registered for the *Introduction to Racing* class. As a result, she completed the program and graduated with a Bachelor of Science degree in Animal Science.

Lovitt took a job with TOC, the Thoroughbred Owners of California. A move to California was both exciting and challenging. Starting a life and career in a new state was a wonderful adventure, and she remained with TOC for the next fourteen years.

It was during Lovitt's time with TOC that Madeline Auerbach began her efforts to find an answer to the problems facing retired racehorses. When CARMA was founded in 2007, it was a committee under the umbrella of TOC. As the need grew for racehorse retirement options, so did CARMA's responsibilities. It became a separate organization in 2011. Lovitt became the executive director.

In more than fourteen years since (as of this writing), CARMA's mission has not changed. It continues to work on behalf of 501(c)(3) charities by helping to fund their efforts to retire or retrain California Thoroughbred racehorses wherever they are located.

The first year of operations saw CARMA providing helpful funding to just eight or nine

Chapter 20 - California Retirement Management Account

charities. As of December 2024, it has awarded $475,000 in grants to twenty-four organizations.

Horses are first accepted into the CARMA Placement Program. There the horse is evaluated for health and fitness and suitability for retraining. Some horses may be deemed as in need of just a life in a sanctuary such as Old Friends Farm or Harmony and Hope Horse Haven. CARMA supports programs for retraining, adoption, therapy, and sanctuary. All funds are donated to programs which have horses that have raced at California major racetracks such as Santa Anita and Del Mar. Because Silver Charm raced in California, he made it possible for Old Friends to receive grants from CARMA.

I find particularly inspiring another service that CARMA provides. The organization works to train owners on how to plan for their horses' retirements. During my interview with Lovitt, she said it had become the norm for owners to plan for retirement before a horse has even started racing. "By and large, owners and trainers do a pretty good job of retiring their horses appropriately," she said.

CHAPTER 21

Retired Racehorse Project

For every horse whose race is done,
Rescue brings hope, a rising sun.
Through tireless work, they find their way,
A second chance, a brighter day.

On October 10, 2024 I went to the Kentucky Horse Park located just outside Lexington, Kentucky. The beautiful, expansive facility with its visitor's center, museum, stables, and arenas was hosting the Thoroughbred Makeover and National Symposium run by the Retired Racehorse Project (RRP). It was an exquisite fall day. Birds were chirping from the many large deciduous trees that still held their leaves. Horses whinnied from stalls. Announcers called out scores over loudspeakers. I walked around, loving being immersed in the horse

Chapter 21 - Retired Racehorse Project

show environment.

In the covered arena, riders in their sequined shirts, cowboy hats and western saddles, competed in the Competitive Trail division. Outside, riders in white breeches, black coats and hard hats warmed up their horses for their time in the dressage arena. In all, riders were competing in ten categories. The one common denominator that one would not see in a typical show: every horse was an off-the-track Thoroughbred!

The Makeover was the culmination of many months of work by trainers registered with the Retired Racehorse Project. The Retired Racehorse Project's mission is to increase the demand for Thoroughbreds beyond racing.

The ten categories are divided into two groups: racehorses and broodmares. The trainers could compete in two of the following categories: Barrel Racing, Competitive Trail, Dressage, Eventing, Field Hunter, Freestyle, Polo, Ranch Work, Show Hunter, and Show Jumper. Freestyle was an interesting category, as the trainers could be completely creative and do whatever they wanted. The 2024 winner dressed as a UPS delivery man and did several tricks with her horse using large boxes as props.

As a thirteen-year-old horse-lover born to a non-horsey family, I dreamt of owning my own horse. While taking lessons at a hunter/jumper barn, I witnessed the popularity of Thoroughbreds. But, as a young girl, I didn't have the money to buy such an expensive horse. Thoroughbreds, in the 1960's were the horse of choice. With what little money I had, I was thrilled to be able to get a young, untrained, Arabian gelding. That wonderful little horse took care of me as we moved up the levels in Pony Club doing dressage and jumping.

With the introduction of European warmbloods a decade or so later, Thoroughbreds began to be replaced in the jumping and dressage arenas.

After a twenty-five year absence from horse ownership and now a married mother of five, my time finally came to get a horse of my own once again. By this time, the price of warmbloods was beyond my reach, but the price of Thoroughbreds, even if never raced, was in my ballpark. Enter Kit, my wonderful, bay Thoroughbred gelding who took me to the dressage championships and all over the Colorado mountain trails.

And I was not the only one to notice the change in the horse show world.

Steuart Pittman, Jr.

Steuart Pittman, Jr. was practically born in the saddle, growing up on the sprawling 550-acre Doden Farm near Davidsonville, Maryland. His childhood was filled with the rhythmic cadence of hoofbeats and the thrill of galloping across open fields. Through Pony Club, he mastered the art of three-day eventing, a demanding sport that tests both horse and rider in dressage, cross-country jumping, and stadium jumping.

But, as it often does, life led him away from the equestrian world for a decade. When Steuart returned in 1990, he dove back into training horses and riders in eventing, dressage, and jumping. Yet,

Chapter 21 - Retired Racehorse Project

something had changed. The sport-horse landscape had shifted, with new breeds rising in popularity—the warmbloods. The warmbloods are a result of breeding hot bloods, Thoroughbreds or Arabians, with cold bloods, the draft breeds. The result is a strong, athletic horse that tends to have a calmer disposition, making it ideal for competition.

Still, through all the trends and transformations, one thing remained unwavering—his deep, abiding love for the Thoroughbred breed.

In the spring of 2009, as president of the Maryland Horse Council, he invited equestrian and equine business consultant Elisabeth McMillan to speak at a seminar. His vision for the meeting was to call attention to the talent being wasted when a Thoroughbred racehorse is retired. He wanted to educate people on where to find them, how to select them, how to train them, and even how to make a business out of retraining and selling them.

Pittman's vision became a reality in 2010 when the Retired Racehorse Project was formed. In 2012, RRP hosted the first 100-day challenge during which four trainers had that short amount of time to retrain an OTTB. Each trainer displayed what his or her horse had accomplished in that period of time at the Pennsylvania Horse World Expo. The Thoroughbred Makeover was born!

The first Thoroughbred Makeover and National Symposium took place at Pimlico Racecourse in 2013. Twenty-six trainers and horses showed their stuff before hundreds of spectators.

By 2015, the Thoroughbred Makeover had grown so much, it became a national event. It was now a competition, offering more than $100,000 in prize money. It was also moved to the Kentucky Horse Park. Each year, more and more people apply to be trainers, and more and more Thoroughbreds are given a second chance.

Tia Jones and Meili

The wind was howling across the prairie when I went to visit trainer Tia Jones in Parker, Colorado. The Continental Divide, visible to the west, glowed white against the bright blue sky, having recently received its first coating of snow. Several horses, of all sizes and colors, roamed along the track system set up around the perimeter of the large pastures.

I parked my car and found Jones in the canvas dome-covered arena. She had been accepted as a trainer for the 2024 Thoroughbred Makeover and had recently purchased a three-year-old bay mare named Napali Coast that Jones calls Meili.

Applying to be a trainer is not an easy undertaking as the RRP is very picky about who it will accept. In addition to a written application, Jones had to send in a video of her working with horses. She is the trainer at Herd of Two Horsemanship and specializes in working with problem horses. She also specializes in starting colts and fillies in a safe, peaceful manner. Much of her own training came from her studies with horsemanship trainers such as Pat Parelli, Buck Branaman, Vaquero horsemen, and others. She also completed all four levels of the Parelli foundational program.

Accepted as a trainer with RRP in February, Tia

Chapter 21 - Retired Racehorse Project

Jones began her search for a Thoroughbred that met the requirements to compete in the Thoroughbred Makeover. The horse had to be a Jockey Club-registered Thoroughbred that marked a workout or race after July 1, 2023 and did not have more than 15 retraining rides prior to December 1, 2023. Nepali Coast met all of those requirements.

Meili was living in Kentucky, so Jones had her sister visit the horse. Her sister is not a horse person, so the best evaluation she could make was to tell Jones that Nepali Coast was really "pleasant and peaceful." That sounded good to Jones. She bought Meili and had her shipped to Colorado.

By the time I met Meili, she had been at Tia Jones' small horse ranch for several weeks. Jones had been doing exclusively groundwork with her, but the day I visited was to be her first time mounting the mare. We were both excited about what was coming.

I watched as Jones did several groundwork exercises. Meili's sweet manner was on display, so Jones decided to move up to the next step. She put a western saddle on the horse. Meili didn't complain. She led her to the mounting block. Meili stood quietly. Jones put her left foot in the stirrup and added weight until she was standing on the stirrup in what is called a "half mount." Meili remained quiet. Jones swung her right leg over the cantle and settled softly into the saddle. With lots of patting and praising, Jones sat on her back. Meili turned her head and looked back at Jones as if to say, "What took you so long?"

The rest of the training session went smoothly

158   *Silver Charm*

with Jones working on walking, halting and turning in both directions—what I call testing the steering and brakes.

Tia Jones originally planned to train Meili and then sell her, following the well-established path offered by the Retired Racehorse Project (RRP). Its program, both at the Makeover event and online, connects trainers with buyers seeking talented retrained horses. But as the months passed, something changed.

Tia Jones working Meili over obstacles
(Photo from Jones, used with permission)

Meili wasn't just another project—she became part of Jones' heart. What started as preparation for

Chapter 21 - Retired Racehorse Project

a competitive trail riding career soon took an unexpected turn. Meili had a natural grace, a rhythmic elegance that whispered of dressage. Intrigued and inspired, Jones sought out a dressage trainer, not just for Meili but for herself as well.

With each lesson, their bond deepened. Every movement, every transition, every challenge strengthened their partnership. The idea of parting ways with Meili faded completely. She wasn't just a competition horse anymore—she was family. And now, with growing excitement, Jones looked ahead to their next big adventure: taking Meili to Kentucky, not as a sale prospect, but as her partner in the sport they were both falling in love with.

We all know that some goals don't work out. I have a favorite author mantra: "When things go wrong in your life, just shout 'Plot Twist' and move on."

Such was the unexpected twist in the journey of Tia Jones and her beloved Meili. The dream of competing at the 2024 Thoroughbred Makeover was within reach—until fate or the hand of God had other plans. A knee injury sidelined Jones, leading to the daunting reality of knee replacement surgery.

But setbacks often come with silver linings. While Jones didn't get to step into the Makeover arena that year, she gained something even more enduring—a steadfast partner for the long haul. Meili, with her elegance and untapped potential, remained by her side, ready to climb the levels of dressage together for years to come.

Their story is a reminder that goals may shift, but true partnerships stand the test of time.

Wishing them both a future filled with grace, growth, and many triumphant rides ahead!

FULL CIRCLE

CHAPTER 22

In Conclusion:

The October sun warmed my back as a gentle breeze only hinted at the coming change of seasons. I leaned against the rail. A few feet away, a man clicked a stopwatch. A shake of his hand and a broad smile told me he was happy with what he saw.

My attention went back to the activity in front of me. Nearly a dozen young Thoroughbreds were going through their morning training exercises on the dry dirt surface at Keeneland Racecourse. Some were walking near the rail where I stood, their exercise riders joking with one another. Down the center of the track, a horse and rider cooled down with a slow canter, the horse's neck gently rounded, the rider standing in her stirrups.

A few minutes later, two young, sleek Thoroughbreds, one chestnut, his copper-colored coat sparkling in the sun, the other a dapple gray with a black mane and tail, sprinted along the rail. Their speed was almost dizzying to watch as they alternately stretched and folded their legs, reaching ever farther, ever faster. Their nostrils were opened wide, sucking in the oxygen their rippling muscles demanded. Their riders' arms pumping with the undulation of their mounts' heads and necks. My own heart pounded with every beat of their hooves.

In my mind's eye, I could envision Silver Charm as one of those young three-year-old colts, his coat a dark gray, not yet faded with age. His tail, the top half black, the lower half silver, flowing out behind him. His ears twisting forward and back, listening for the approach of any horse who dared to challenge him...and hoping they would try.

Truly, Silver Charm has led a charmed life, a beloved champion.

My attention focused back on the Thoroughbreds in front of me. The elegant, sculpted bodies glistening with sweat, their long, thin legs, seemingly too fine to carry the weight of their muscled bodies, prancing in the soft dirt, their lovely heads tossing. They were truly a joy to behold. And I wondered as I looked at each one: What would the future bring for them?

I knew their time on the track, doing what they were born to do, doing what they love to do, would be but a short season of their lives. I prayed for their health and safety, knowing how many injuries might await them and hoping they would be few and minor. And then I prayed they, like Silver Charm, would have a life's tapestry woven by people who loved them.

For a year, I researched the life of Silver Charm. As I did so, my search led me to many people and horses whose lives connected and influenced his—the weavers. They put the charm in Silver Charm's life.

Chapter 22 - In Conclusion:

Happily, there are now many old friends who are weaving bright, cheerful colors into so many racehorse's tapestries. Through the dedication of countless compassionate individuals, healthy Thoroughbred racehorses are being given a second chance and a new purpose, while those who are aging or injured find comfort in well-deserved retirement homes.

And so, I close this book with a heartfelt toast to the racehorses, the backyard ponies, the dependable trail horses, the working ranch horses, the fancy show horses:

Here's to the extraordinary horses— The ones who are forever woven into our lives, leaving hoofprints on our hearts.

FINAL NOTES
ACKNOWLEDGEMENTS:

History that is not recorded is lost forever. I hope that my efforts to compile the information about Silver Charm and the Old Friends who save the Thoroughbreds will serve to keep this part of history alive for those who come after us. While many of the people who were weavers on Silver Charm's tapestry have passed on, several are still in his life. I am deeply indebted to Michael Blowen, Gary Stevens, and Sandy Hatfield, important people in Silver Charm's life, who gave me so much of their time as they shared their knowledge of and experiences with such a special horse. It was a great privilege to be able to talk with them for many hours and record their memories.

Kelly Coffman and Roda Ferraro were priceless resources. As the research librarians at the Keeneland Library in Kentucky, they provided me with dozens of articles and photographs about Silver Charm.

It was a pleasure to meet Carmen Forshaw of the Thoroughbred Aftercare Alliance, Kate Anderson, Olivia Murray, and Tori Donovan at Center for Racehorse Retraining, and Tia Jones of the Retired Racehorse Project. I truly appreciate their generosity in sharing their experiences and allowing me to see them in action. Their dedication to retired racehorses and their commitment to providing these horses with new career opportunities through these vital programs is both inspiring and commendable. I am grateful to Lucinda Lovitt and Ruth Plenty for allowing me to interview them and learn about what they do to save the Thoroughbreds.

I am also grateful to my beta readers who read through various drafts of this book. Their feedback is invaluable as I strive to make this book both fun and educational. Thank you, Karen Schick and Lynn Johnson. I am grateful for the careful proofreading provide by Sophia Barsuhn.

Lastly, this book would never get done without the encouragement and prodding of my editor, Denny Dressman. Denny is a former sports editor of the *Rocky Mountain News*, an author of many non-fiction books about sports figures and other subjects, and, as a special bonus, grew up in Kentucky where he developed an interest in horse racing. As a result, he was excited about this idea when I presented it to him and was eager to help me all along the way.

Cover painting by Johnny Deemer. Thank you for sharing your talents.

As my granddaughter said: "Teamwork makes the dreamwork!"

EDITOR'S NOTE: The poignant poems that so appropriately introduce each section of *SILVER CHARM - And the Old Friends Who Save the Thoroughbreds* are the original work of the author, M.J. Evans. They demonstrate another dimension of her writing talent as a weaver of perceptive equine books.

FINAL NOTES

APPENDIX

Three Chimneys Press Release

(Copied from an image sent from the Keeneland Library files)

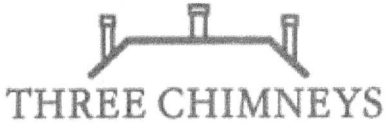

THREE CHIMNEYS
The Idea is Excellence.

From: Margaret Layton
To: Thoroughbred Times
For Release
July 18, 1999

For Further Information:
Robert Clay or Dan Rosenberg

CHAMPION SILVER CHARM TO THREE CHIMNEYS FARM

LEXINGTON, KY...Bob and Beverly Lewis announced today that Silver Charm, Kentucky Derby (G1) and Preakness (G1) winner and 3-year-old champion of 1997 who has amassed earnings of $6.94 million, will stand at Mr. & Mrs. Robert N. Clay's Three Chimneys Farm.

Robert Clay said that the stud fee for Silver Charm, a great favorite of the racing public, will be $25,000 guaranteed live foal and confirmed that the horse will be owned by a partnership involving the Lewises and Clay.

"We're extremely pleased to have our near-Triple Crown winner standing alongside noted Triple Crown victor Seattle Slew," comment Bob Lewis. "Three Chimneys has been interested in this horse for a longtime, and we're glad it's worked out for him to be there."

"We're looking forward not only to stand Silver Charm—a horse of amazing ability and consistency and an interesting stallion pedigree, but to welcoming his fans. It is a lot like having Seattle Slew—a great privilege and responsibility, and we're honored the Lewises have chosen Three Chimneys," said Robert Clay.

Final Notes - APPENDIX

Clay noted that there are pedigree similarities between Silver Charm and Seattle Slew (they share the same broodmare sire of Poker, and Hail to Reason occupies the same position in each horse's pedigree—being the broodmare sire of each horse's sire), and that the Buckpasser element in Silver Charm's pedigree will be an asset in the horse's stallion career.

"Silver Charm is the best Buckpasser-line runner ever," explained Three Chimneys matings advisor Ed Anthony. "He provides a rare opportunity for "sex balance" inbreeding to Buckpasser, damsire of top stallions like Believe it, El Gran Senor, Miswaki, Private Account, Seeking the Gold, Slew o'Gold, Wavering Monarch and Woodman."

Silver Charm retires as the third richest racehorse in history, with earnings of $6,944,369. He was the champion Three-Year-old colt of 1997, topping Deputy Commander and Touch Gold in the balloting. When he won the Dubai Cup, he was the first Kentucky Derby winner to race overseas since Carry Back in 1961 and Omaha in 1935. In 24 career starts, he was noted for many desperately close finishes and ways only once out of the money until his last two outings (the Dubai Cup and Steven Foster Handicap of 1999—both of which he won in 1998).

Silver Charm has been widely credited with helping bring Thoroughbred racing back into the national spotlight, and he developed a legion of fans with his game performances. Twice he was caught off-guard in the closing strides of races that would, if won, have made him the leading money-winning horse of all time. In the 1997 Belmont, Touch Gold swept by on the far outside to edge Silver Charm by three-quarters of a length and deprive him of the $5 million Triple Crown bonus. In the $5 million Breeder's Cup Classic of 1998, Awesome Again closed on the far inside of Silver Charm to win by the same margin.

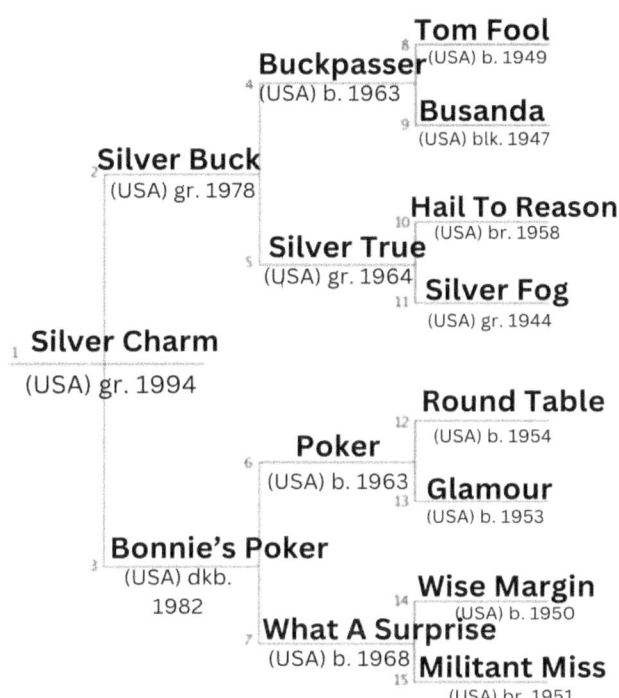

NOTE: Busanda's sire was War Admiral whose sire was Man O'War

Silver Charm's Pedigree
(from Pedigreequery.com)

Runner's Story
by Ruth Plenty

SUCCESSFUL RUNNER Celebrates HIS 15th Birthday February 02.

Runner said he's pretty certain Groundhog did not see his shadow this morning because he wouldn't come out in today's weather. The light drizzle two days ago was indeed a drizzle compared to the storm that moved in around 2 this morning. Actually, it was one of the best lay down and roll days he's had in quite some time.

From here on I'll let Runner tell his story: I was born in Kentucky February 2, 2009. September 2010 at 19 months of age I was entered in the Keeneland Yearling Sale and sold for $80,000. And the next morning my first day of a racing career began. I was a big colt, and my owners took their time getting me ready for my first race.

My first race on January 14, 2013, Maiden Special Weight, I finished third. February 17th, I finished Second. After three more races at Gulfstream Park with 2nd and two 3rd place finishes, I transferred to New York. On June 20th at Belmont Park, I came in second. THEN, July 11, 2014 I won my first race. That was the last Maiden Special Weight I would ever be able to run. At Saratoga on September 1st, I weakened a little, but I still came in

3rd. After that, I took some well-deserved time off from racing. July 29, 2015, I ran in a Claiming race, came in Second and now had new owners. Once more I was given time off and on April 23, 2016, in another Claiming race, I won my second race.

On June 2016, at Churchill Downs, in another Claiming race, I won my third race and once more I had new owners. And just like that, one day I was in Kentucky and the next I was in California. July 16, 2016, opening day at Del Mar Thoroughbred Club, was my last race. X-rays revealed fractures in the left and right front sesamoid with other fractures in the left and right front. Out of ten horses in that race I still came in 7th. From January 1, 2013, to my last race July 16, 2016, I ran in 12 races ... I brought home three Wins, four Seconds, and four Thirds; my total earnings: $132,685.00

My owners spoke with CARMA, California Retirement Management Account, who took me into their Placement Program lay-up facility and would find me an aftercare home once I completed my recovery.

My future activities were to be very limited. Nine months lay-up, now without pain medications, I had graduated from a 12x12 stall to roam freely in a larger paddock. CARMA Placement Program felt Sanctuary placement was my best option.

Just like claiming races, I was about to have a

new owner. Monday, June 12th at 3:20 that morning I arrived at Harmony and Hope Horse Haven. By nine I felt like I'd lived here forever.

I learned the human was called 'The Old Mare'. About 6 AM she came back to my paddock, looked at me a couple minutes, then said, "Hello Handsome." So that afternoon when she said she'd been told I would need some ground schooling to learn how to behave like a gentleman, I said "No, that's not true." All these years later, she still says, "Hello Handsome" and rubs my face. And, then she tells me "You are such a gentleman." I wait for those words before I start eating my hay and grains she has just brought me. I'm great having my annual leg x-rays, great with the farrier; a bit fussy about vaccinations but The Old Mare says, "stop that." So, I do just what she says. After all, I'm handsome and such a gentleman.

Listing of 2024 TAA Accredited Aftercare facilities (TAA website)

ACTT Naturally, Inc.
After the Homestretch - Arizona
After The Races
After The Races NY Inc.
Akindale Thoroughbred Rescue
Beyond The Roses Equine Rescue & Retirement
Bowman Second Chance Thoroughbred Adoption
Bright Futures Farm, Inc.
Brook Hill Retirement Center for Horses
CANTER California
CANTER Kentucky
CANTER Michigan
Caribbean Thoroughbred Aftercare
Center for Racehorse Retraining
Central Kentucky Riding For Hope
Central Virginia Horse Rescue
Champions Retreat
Circle A Home for Horses
Dale and Patti Shirley Equine Encore Foundation
Days End Farm Horse Rescue
Desert Oasis Rescue LLC
Down The Stretch Ranch
Equestrian Inc.

Equine Advocates Inc.
Equine Rescue & Adoption Foundation
Equine Rescue of Aiken
Final Furlong, Inc.
Finger Lakes Thoroughbred Adoption Program
Friends of Ferdinand
Galloping Out
Glen Ellen Vocational Academy, Inc.
Harmony and Hope Horse Haven, Inc.
Healing Arenas
Heart of Phoenix Equine Rescue
Hidden Acres Rescue for Thoroughbreds
Hidden Pond Farm Equine Rescue
Hope After Racing Thoroughbreds
Hope for Horses, Inc.
Hope's Legacy
Horse and Hound Rescue Foundation
Illinois Equine Humane Center
James River Horse Foundation
Kentucky Equine Adoption Center
Lollypop Farm
LoneStar Outreach to Place Ex-Racers
LongRun Thoroughbred Retirement Society
Lucky Orphans Horse Rescue
MidAtlantic Horse Rescue Inc.
NEER North
New Beginnings Thoroughbreds, Inc.

New Stride Thoroughbred Adoption Society
New Vocations Racehorse Adoption Program
Old Friends Equine Retirement
Our Mims Retirement Haven
Out Side In, Inc.
Racing For Home, Inc.
Redwings Horse Sanctuary
Remember Me Rescue
ReRun, Inc.
Rising Starr Horse Rescue Corporation
Run for the Ribbons Inc.
Sandia Creek Ranch Auxiliary Foundation
Second Call Thoroughbred Adoption Program
Second Chance Thoroughbreds, Inc.
Second Stride, Inc
Second Wind Thoroughbred Project, Inc.
Secretariat Center
South Florida SPCA
Square Peg Foundation
The Exceller Fund, Inc.
The Foxie G Foundation
The Harry A. Biszantz Memorial Center for Thoroughbred Retirement, Tranquility Farm
The Susan S. Donaldson Foundation (Mereworth Farm, LLC)
Therapeutic Horses of Saratoga
This Old Horse
Thoroughbred Athletes, Inc.
Thoroughbred Placement Resources, Inc.

Thoroughbred Retirement Foundation

Thoroughbred Retirement Network of Louisiana

TRRAC Thoroughbred Retirement, Rehabilitation, and Careers

United Pegasus Foundation

Virginia Thoroughbred Project

Win Place Home, Inc.

FINAL NOTES

Bibliography

Interviews:

Michael Blowen – Founder of Old Friends Farm

Gary Stevens – Silver Charm's jockey

Sandy Hatfield – Stallion Manager at Three Chimneys Farm when Silver Charm stood at stud

Carmen Forshaw – Program Coordinator at New Stride Thoroughbred Adoption Society

Kate Anderson - Executive Director of the Center for Racehorse Retraining.

Tia Jones – Trainer at Herd of Two Horsemanship

Ruth Plenty – Founder of Harmony and Hope Horse Haven

Lucinda Lovitt – Executive Director of CARMA

Books:

Baffert, Bob and Haskin, Steve, *Dirt Road to the Derby*, 1999, The BloodHorse, Inc.

Capone, Rick, *History of Old Friends,* 2014, The History Press

Stevens, Gary, *The Perfect Ride,* 2002, Citadel Press

Articles:

"A Stable Affair for 56 Years," Aug. 20, 2021, *Chicago Tribune*

Angst, Frank, May 2020, "The Charmed One," *BloodHorse*, pg. 42-43

Angst, Frank, May 2022, "Still Charming," *BloodHorse,* pg. 70-79

Bayer, Barbara, Dec. 16, 2003, "The Search for Ferdinand," *BloodHorse*

Blowen, Michael, Mar. 1, 2001, "Retired Racehorses Sent to Prison for Home Stretch— Inmates Learn Skills, Animals Thrive from Care," *The Boston Globe*

"CA Sire Unusual Heat Hist Earnings Milestone," Feb. 29, 2016, *BloodHorse*

Cain, Gleyne, Oct. 31, 2004, "Silver Charm to Stand in Japan," *Daily Racing Form*, pg. 14

Cochran, Caroline, April 29, 2024, "Lasix (Furosemide) for Horses with Bleeders: Uses, Doses and Side Effects, *M.B. Madbarn*

Dempsy, Jane, May 1, 2017, "History of the

Final Notes - Bibliography   185

Garland of Roses for the Kentucky Derby Winner," *Kentucky Derby Tours Blog*

Dixon, Tom, Nov. 13, 2014, "Alydar's Final Hours," *BloodHorse*

Dorso, Joseph, May 12, 1997, "Fewer Challenges for Silver Charm," *The New York Times*

Duckworth, Amanda, Sep. 25, 2024, "Silver Charm, the Horse Who Made Me Fall in Love With Racing," *Thoroughbred Racing Commentary*

"Eclipse—One of the Greatest Racehorses," Feb. 16, 2016, *Honest Betting Reviews*

Eddy, Mary, Dec. 4, 2024, "Akindale Thoroughbred Aftercare Carries on Legacy of Hall of Famer John Hettinger," *Paulick Report*

Ehalt, Bob, Jan. 25, 2021, "Bob and Beverly Lewis: Beloved Racing Royalty," *The Sport*

Friedman, Jay, Dec. 1999, "Best of the Century," *The Florida Horse*, pg. 54

Haskin, Steve, Aug. 4, 2007, "Crowd Charmer," *BloodHorse,* pg. 4180

"Horse Advocate John Hettinger Dies," Dec. 6, 2008, *BloodHorse*

Hovdey, Jay, Sept. 21, 1996, "Team Lewis," *BloodHorse*

"How One Horse and One Owner Changed Thoroughbred Aftercare in California," July 11, 2020, *18/18/carma4horses.org*

LaMarra, Tom, June 2, 2007, "Full Crop," *BloodHorse*, pg. 3120

Layton, Margaret, April 29, 2015, "Silver Charm Arrives at Three Chimneys in 1999," *Rosecrest Farm*

Paulick, Ray, Feb. 6, 1999, Port O'Mandella, *BloodHorse pg.* 852 and 853

Paulick, Ray, July 25, 2003, "Death of a Derby Winner: Slaughterhouse Likely Fate for Ferdinand," *BloodHorse*

Paulick, Ray, Dec. 2, 2014, "Back Home Again: Silver Charm Arrives at Old Friends," *The Paulick Report*

Ross, Daniel, Nov. 15, 2019, "Q and A with Madeline Auerbach," *Thoroughbred Daily News*

Simon, Mary, Oct. 29, 2014, "Silver Charm Returns from Japan to Go to Old Friends," *DRF*

"Unusual Heat Dies at 27," May 17, 2017, *BloodHorse*

Voss, Natalie, May 11, 2017, "I'm Afraid That Something is Going to Happen: Stevens Wishes Derby Field Were Smaller, *Paulick Report*

Whyno, Stephen, May 23, 2023, "Jockey Suicides Bring Attention to Stress and Mental Health Concerns of the Job," *PBS News*

Websites:

Blue Horse Charities: https://www.bluehorsecharities.org

California Retirement Management Account: https://www.carma4horses.org

Center for Racehorse Retraining: https://www.wyomingottb.org

Churchill Downs: https://www.churchilldowns.com

Final Notes - Bibliography

Harmony and Hope Horse Haven: https://www.harmonyandhopehorsehaven.org

Herd of Two Horsemanship: https://tiajoneshorsemanship.com

Keeneland: https://www.keeneland.com

Keeneland Library: https://www.keeneland.com/keeneland-library

New Stride Thoroughbred Adoption Society: https://www.newstride.com/

Old Friends: https/oldfriendsequine.org

Pedigreequery.com

Retired Racehorse Project: https://www.therrp.org

Thoroughbred Aftercare Alliance: https://www.thoroughbredaftercare.org

Three Chimneys: https://www.threechimneys.com

About the Author

M.J. Evans is the award-winning author of more than twenty published works spanning middle-grade, young adult, and adult fiction, as well as a selection of picture books. Her writing often explores themes centered around horses and equine fantasy, reflecting a lifelong passion for these remarkable animals. A graduate of Oregon State University and a former educator with experience teaching both middle and high school students, Ms. Evans brings both educational insight and storytelling flair to her work. She resides in beautiful Colorado with her husband,

Tom, where they enjoy the company of their horses and standard poodle. She is the proud mother of five and grandmother of thirteen.

The photo depicts the author on her Thoroughbred, Kit.

M.J. Evans was the recipient of the 2024 Colorado Authors League Lifetime Achievement Award.

Literary awards include:
Chanticleer International Book Awards
Readers' Favorite International Awards
Eric Hoffer Awards
Nautilus Awards
Literary Classics awards
Feathered Quill Book Awards
Purple Dragonfly Awards
Royal Dragonfly Awards
Page Turner Award
Next Generation Award
Global Book Awards
CIPA Evvy Book Awards
Pinnacle Book Achievement Awards
Incipere Book Awards
International Impact Book Awards
Maincrest Media Book Awards
Book Excellence Awards
Mom's Choice Awards

Visit her website to learn more about the author and her books.

If you enjoyed this book, please take a minute to post a short review on Amazon. That helps others find the book as well.

You can contact M.J. Evans on her website: **www.dancinghorsepress.com** She loves to receive letters, and she always writes back!

Follow her on social media:
Goodreads:
https://www.goodreads.com/author/show/4496514.MJ Evans
Bookbub:
https://www.bookbub.com/profile/m-j-evans

Amazon:
https://www.amazon.com/stores/M.-J.-Evans/author/B004GMS014

Instagram:
https://www.instagram.com/mjevansbooks

Facebook:
https://www.facebook.com/profile.php?id=61553522941532

Join her email list for occasional updates on new releases and receive a FREE PDF of a short Christmas story.

Email her at **mjevansbtm@gmail.com** and put "Join email list" in the subject line

Read more Award-Winning Titles by M.J. Evans:

Novels:
Coal Dust and Dreams
Finding Fionn
The Stallion and His Peculiar Boy
In the Heart of a Mustang
The Sand Pounder
PINTO!
North Mystic
Mr. Figgletoes' Toy Emporium

Biography:
Silver Charm

Fantasy Series:
The Mist Trilogy-
Behind the Mist
Mists of Darkness
The Rising Mist

The Centaur Chronicles-
The Stone of Mercy
The Stone of Courage
The Stone of Integrity
The Stone of Wisdom

Picture Books:
Percy-The Racehorse Who Didn't Like to Run
The Skullington Family Series-
Boney Fingers
Bone Appetit
School is a Grave Mistake
Skeletons in the Closet

Equestrian Trail Guidebooks for Colorado

Riding Colorado
Riding Colorado II
Riding Colorado III
Riding Colorado and Beyond

All titles are available on the website:
www.dancinghorsepress.com
And wherever books are sold.

www.ingramcontent.com/pod-product-compliance
Lightning Source LLC
Chambersburg PA
CBHW071239070526
44583CB00017B/2248